JOHN DEERE
TRACTORS

Scott Webb

Photography by Andy Kraushaar

Voyageur Press

First published in 2007 by Voyageur Press, an imprint of MBI Publishing Company, Galtier Plaza, Suite 200, 380 Jackson Street, St. Paul, MN 55101 USA

The information in this book is true and complete to the best of our knowledge. All recommendations are made without any guarantee on the part of the author or Publisher, who also disclaim any liability incurred in connection with the use of this data or specific details.

This publication has not been prepared, approved, or licensed by Deere & Company. We recognize, further, that some words, model names, and designations mentioned herein are the property of the trademark holder. We use them for identification purposes only. This is not an official publication.

Voyageur Press titles are also available at discounts in bulk quantity for industrial or sales-promotional use. For details write to Special Sales Manager at MBI Publishing Company, Galtier Plaza, Suite 200, 380 Jackson Street, St. Paul, MN 55101 USA.

To find out more about our books, join us online at www.voyageurpress.com.

Library of Congress Cataloging-in-Publication Data

Webb, Scott, 1962-
  John Deere tractors /Scott Webb; photography by Andy Kraushaar.
    p. cm.
  ISBN-13: 978-0-7603-3152-1 (softbound)
  ISBN-10: 0-7603-3152-9 (softbound)
  1. John Deere tractors--History. I. Kraushaar, Andy, 1953-
II. Title.
TL233.6.J64W43 2007
629.225'2--dc22

                                        2007018076

Editor: Leah Noel
Designer: James Kegley

Printed in China

About the Author
Scott Webb has been an engineer and worked as an editor and writer in the agriculture and construction equipment industry for nearly a decade. The author of MBI Publishing Company's *Tractor Pull!*, he also was a major contributor to *The Caterpillar Century* and many Caterpillar and John Deere calendars. He currently is splitting his time between New Zealand and Madison, Wisconsin.

About the Photographer
Photographer Andy Kraushaar has been capturing the glory of John Deere and Farmall tractors for more than a decade. His work has appeared in several MBI Publishing Company titles, including *Farmall Letter Series Tractors*, *Toy Farm Tractors*, and the 2006 and 2007 John Deere Tractor-a-Day calendars. He lives in Madison, Wisconsin.

Cover
Main: The Model 8100, produced from 1994 to 1998 at John Deere's Waterloo, Iowa, plant. *Inset, from left:* Model AOS, Model H, and Model BI.

Back cover
A 1929 Model GP, a Model 4020, and a Model HWH.

Frontis Piece
A variant of the immensely successful Model A, the Model AR ("R" for regular) was a fixed-tread version of the base model. This tractor was built in 1952. Production of the model stopped the following year.

Title pages
Based on the Model B, the BN was marketed as a "garden tractor" to row-crop farmers who didn't have the acreage to demand the higher horsepower A. Its distinctive feature was a single front wheel, which ran between the crop rows. Pictured here is a 1935 version, complete with steel wheels.

Table of Contents
The John Deere Model 730 sold more than 29,000 units between 1958 and 1961. The 730 was the original flexible-fuel machine; it could be ordered as a gas, LPG, diesel, or all-fuel tractor.

Contents

In the Blacksmith's Workshop

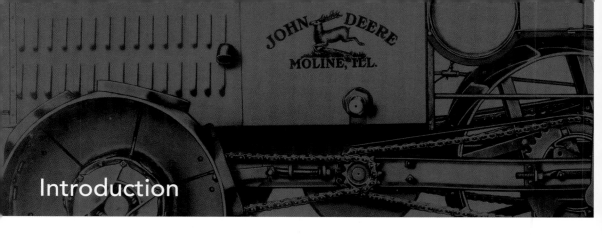

Introduction

It must have seemed like any other metalworker's shop in northern Illinois in the 1830s—a plank-clad shed, rather cramped, but undoubtedly quaint by the standards of today. The locals in Grand Detour probably passed it with no more notice than the general store or the tannery or the saloon. They could not have imagined that one day 33,000 skilled employees would be working for their local blacksmith.

What was not apparent at a glance was this blacksmith's deep-seated drive to improve his trade. Such was his nature. When John Deere looked at a piece of metalwork, his eye caught the place feature could be made better.

And when he looked out across the fields beyond his town and saw his customers struggling to draw plows across the sticky, black Midwestern soil—which caked and clogged and confounded their passage—he saw something wrong that had to be made right.

The question of how to improve farming procedures was still in the back of his mind when he came across a broken steel blade at a friend's sawmill. It was just lying on the ground, discarded, but somehow it drew him closer. He picked it up and examined its flat, shiny surface. He then forced the steel down into the ground, moved it forward a few inches with a curving motion, and pulled it up.

It came out clean. John Deere didn't know at that moment that his idea would result in widely popular green farm machines. He probably just sensed that he was really on to something. Soon his steel plow business was up and running, and there was no doubt that the product would be a success.

In a little over 10 years, John Deere relocated his operation to Moline, Illinois, with its Mississippi River access to new markets and where the company headquarters remain to this day.

A portrait of John Deere, taken from the years when his success as company founder was assured. Deere's characteristic drive and commitment are evident in this photograph. *Voyageur Press Archives*

Fifteen years after selling his first plow out of his blacksmith shop, John Deere was making 4,000 plows a year in a new Moline, Illinois, location. *Voyageur Press Archives*

He was now making over 1,000 plows a year and was a wealthy man.

After 15 years of business, his annual output was more than 4,000 plows—every farmer in the vast flatlands between the Alleghenies and the Rockies had heard of John Deere.

But it would take another century before the blacksmith's fame would reach a unique pinnacle among icons of our culture—when the man became known not just by his hame but a color, Deere Green.

As the nineteenth century passed its midpoint, John Deere had a large company to run, and, to his relief, his son, Charles, was showing both an aptitude and willingness to work for the family business. All sorts of new machines were being created to multiply the harvest and speed farm labor, and the Deeres focused their efforts on adding specialty plows and contemporary cultivators and harrows to their original line.

Steadily, the company grew. There was no great secret to their success; the Deeres cared about quality, and their products did not disappoint in the field. In 1868, father and son decided to incorporate. With a capitalization of $150,000, they launched the company as its own entity, under the name that stands to this day, Deere & Company.

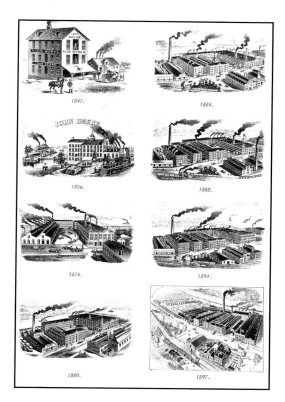

This series of lithographs shows the Deere & Company from 1847 to 1897. The new factory in Moline, Illinois, is shown in 1847, the year it began production, and subsequent renderings display the company's expanding size and distribution facilities. *Voyageur Press Archives*

In 1886, at the age of 82, John Deere passed away, leaving a thriving farm machinery business firmly under the command of his son. John had proved himself an uncommonly good organizer and a man dedicated to simple, steady improvement. He'd given the legend its name and written its first chapter, but it would take decades of imagination and effort to make Deere & Company what it is today. That would require the efforts of businessmen and blacksmiths yet to be.

At the dawn of the twentieth century, the American farming community was in profound

Some of the hundreds of thousands of workers who have contributed to the legendary company started by John Deere. Shown here are builders of the Model D. This photo depicts the Waterloo plant on a workday in 1924. Note the use of horses for moving materials within the plant and daylight for illumination. An overhead shaft supplies belt power for factory tools and machines. *Voyageur Press Archives*

transition. For thousands of years, humans had provided the brains, and animals the muscle, to gather the harvest. The change to mechanized farming was more than a financial gamble for farmers; it was a wrenching conversion to an entirely new way of life. They knew how to handle a plow horse, but replacing a flywheel was beyond their ken.

Tractors were commercially available in the 1890s, but there were not many buyers—and Deere & Company was not very interested in making them just yet. Implements such as threshers and cultivators were the proven market,

where Deere & Company concentrated its efforts.

By 1912, however, it was becoming obvious that the tractor was here to stay. And the new president of Deere & Company, Charles Deere's son-in-law, William Butterworth, decided it was a market the company could no longer ignore. With some trepidation, he gave the go-ahead for engineer C. H. Melvin to develop a prototype under the Deere company banner.

It made a lot of sense from a marketing standpoint. The company's products had been pulled behind horses for decades. But modern plows were being pulled behind tractors in ever-increasing

This photo perfectly captures the transition of animal power to internal combustion—the eventual legacy of Deere & Company—that took place over decades. These horses work alongside a 1935 John Deere Model BN and thresher. Although rubber tires were available and common by the time this photo was taken, this farmer chose steel wheels and deep lugs. *Voyageur Press Archives*

numbers. If Deere's customers were going to its competitors to buy a tractor, might they start getting implements there as well?

Unfortunately, Deere's first effort in motive power was something of a failure. In plowing mode, the machine used a backward-tricycle arrangement, with the farmer sitting well aft of the contraption, and the front two wheels leading. When pulling anything else, the machine went the other direction, with the single-wheel leading and the farmer sitting in front. This bidirectional tractor was prone to breakdown, and an expensive lesson for Butterworth and Deere.

With newspapers filled with stories of failing tractor companies, the project lagged. It wasn't until 1914 that the board of directors again took up the issue, having been spurred by the imperious need to enter the ever-growing tractor market. It was with this second attempt at a viable tractor that the Deere tractor line was born. A formal directive was bestowed upon Joseph Dain Senior, whose company, Dain Manufacturing, had been acquired by Deere only four years previously, to "report to the Executive Committee whether or not a tractor could be built to sell at about $700."

It could, Dain concluded, and on June 24, 1914, the board gave its approval for the design and development of "an efficient small plow tractor . . . under the auspices of Mr. Dain and the Experimental Department."

Dain's successful design used the backward-tricycle configuration of the earlier Melvin prototype, but featured many improvements, and it was a primarily forward-driving tractor. It had a four-cylinder engine, iron wheels, and chains to connect the powerplant to the wheels—an important innovation.

Unfortunately, the cost of building the tractor rose well beyond the $700 benchmark the board had imposed. While this caused some consternation, the number one design imperative had been met; the tractor was reliable. So the tools were ordered to begin production of the first tractor to bear the John Deere name. A production run of exactly 10 machines was ordered.

More improvements followed, and by 1917, the seventh model design included ball and roller bearings, heavier drive chains, and a much more durable gear transmission, which ran submerged in oil. This newer version impressed management, and a full production run of 100 machines was ordered.

It was clear at this point that the company was in the tractor business to stay, and new facilities would be necessary. As the board scanned the map of the upper Mississippi valley, it was drawn to a little town in Iowa just 100 miles west of Moline, where there was already a company putting out a fine tractor in its own right. In the Waterloo Gasoline Engine Company, Deere executives saw the facilities and know-how to give their tractor business the boost it needed. Soon the Waterloo Boys, both the tractor and the men making it, were celebrated members of the Deere family.

Model As lined up in model year succession, from 1934 to 1938. As a successful inventor of plows and builder of an implement company, John Deere and his company eventually became synonymous with tractors, old and new, and traditional farming virtues.

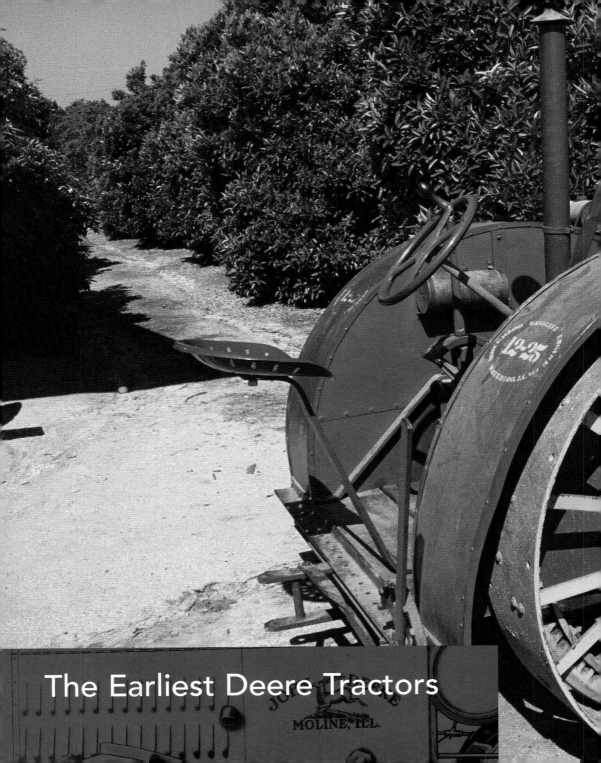

The Earliest Deere Tractors

This Waterloo Boy Model N tractor displays a number of quaint tractor features of its day, including a kerosene fuel tank mounted high up front and iron-spoked wheels. The Model N was a very successful tractor, selling 21,392 units between 1917 and 1924. In 1921, the tractor sold for the steep sum of $1,050.
Hans Halberstadt

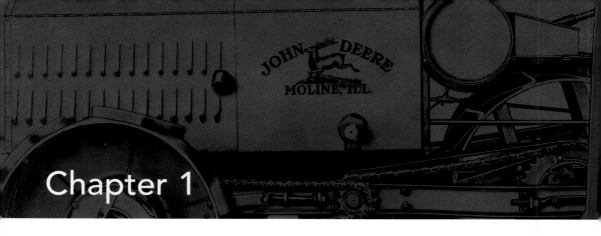

Chapter 1

When Deere & Company bought the Waterloo Gasoline Engine Company on March 14, 1918, the Iowa tractor manufacturer had already been in business for over 25 years. Its assets, as well as its status as an established tractor maker, demanded the substantial purchase price of $2.35 million.

The company was established in the early 1890s by John Froelich, a High Plains thresherman with an eye for invention. He regularly traveled to South Dakota for seasonal threshing work, and in the late summer of 1892 he brought with him an engine to power his thresher: a one-cylinder Van Duzen with a 14x14-inch bore and stroke.

At the time, stationary engines powering threshers were not outlandish on the prairie. They were set up on a solid foundation, and power was transmitted by belts and pulleys to the thresher, which was fed by farmhands. The engine itself was cooled by water from a local source, which was simply pumped through an engine jacket and then poured out on the ground.

Froelich's tractor engine, however, could move around on wheels under its own power. It was the first apparatus known to do so in both the forward and rearward directions. He solved the mobile cooling problem by circulating the water coolant through a wide, shallow pan where it passed a series of baffles, transferring heat to the ambient air by convection and evaporation.

The machine must have made an impression, because when Froelich got back from South Dakota he was contacted by S. G. Steward, a farm equipment dealer in Waterloo who had heard of the invention and wanted a closer look. In December 1892, Froelich brought his machine to Waterloo, and Steward and Froelich were in business.

Froelich was with the company for only three years. He was an inventor; the constraints of running a business held little interest for him. With Froelich's departure, the company focused on its most marketable product, stationary power units, for which it found an irresistible name: Waterloo Boys.

Even with solid sales, however, by 1913 the Waterloo Gasoline Engine Company had reached the same conclusion as Deere & Company, 100 miles to the east in Moline: While stationary engines still had farming applications, pulling tractors were the future of farming. They could do anything a stationary engine could do, but they didn't need horses to haul them around.

With this in mind, the company modified its Waterloo Boy, and after a number of iterations, produced the Waterloo Boy Model R in 1914. Unlike its predecessors, this tractor used a side-by-side, two-cylinder design and emitted the distinctive popping sound that would become a signature for the Deere brand to come, eventually helping to earn the grand moniker, "Johnny Popper." The Model R needed gasoline to get started, but once it was going, the fuel line switched to kerosene.

This tractor sold more than 8,000 units in 12 different styles—quite a feat for a three-year run. It was replaced in 1917 by the Model N, which added a number of features, including a second forward gear, enabling the new machine to reach a swift top speed of three miles per hour. Heavy chains drew back either end of the forward axle for steering, an arrangement familiar to modern-day soapbox derby entrants.

In that same year, 1917, the United States entered the war in Europe. Huge quantities of equipment and supplies began crossing the Atlantic to aid America's allies, and some of those shipping convoys contained Waterloo Boy tractors, bound for England.

With a large percentage of English manpower in the trenches in France, the new laborsaving tractors were critical to maintaining food production. These vitally important machines were brought to the Overtime Farm Tractor Company in London's East End, repainted, and distributed throughout the countryside as Overtime Rs and Overtime Ns.

Their performance and dependability were part of the decisive push from America, which helped end the four-year stalemate in France and bring World War I to a close in late 1918.

As the decade came to a close and American soldiers returned home, the Waterloo Gasoline Engine Company completed its integration into Deere & Company. Together, they were poised to become a formidable competitor in the new and growing tractor business.

The Waterloo Boy Engine Company first produced stationary engines to bring mechanized power to America's farms in the early 1900s, but soon realized that engines mounted on moving chassis were the wave of the future.

A John Deere Dain all-wheel-drive tractor appears as it did when it was sold in 1918. The Dain was the first tractor made by Deere & Company, built just before the purchase of the Waterloo Gasoline Traction Engine Company. It had a three-wheel, backward-tricycle design and front-wheel steering. Only two of these tractors are known to exist. *Randy Leffingwell*

Schematic for the all-wheel-drive Dain. Note the bicycle-style chain, powering all wheels with a common shaft and uncomfortable-looking iron seat. Engineers simply found the largest man at the office and used his seat for the casting. *Voyageur Press Archives*

A Dain at work in a muddy field, pulling a plow, on which a traditional handle can be seen. This picture illustrates a sea change in farming methods in the 1920s. New technology had been introduced and was being tested. The horse and mule were starting to be replaced, which eventually changed the design of the plow. *Voyageur Press Archives*

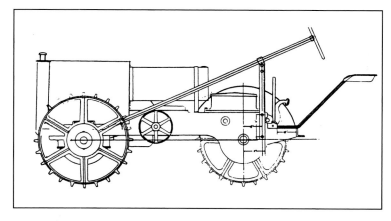

An early sketch of the all-wheel-drive Dain. At this point in the early art of tractor design, many different configurations of wheels and steering were attempted. Note the difference between the flywheel as envisioned in this early sketch and the actual flywheel built (see top photo on p. 16). *Voyageur Press Archives*

An excellent replica of
an 1892 John Froelich
self-propelled gasoline
tractor. Froelich used a
Van Duzen engine
perched above a simple
wood frame. It was the
first tractor to have
the capability for
self-propulsion both
forward and backward.
Randy Leffingwell

An early sketch of the
Froelich tractor. Note
the changes in the
flywheel and the lugs
from the previous photo.
This machine was
intended primarily to
power itself to the
workplace, where it
could pump water or
drive a thresher.
Voyageur Press Archives

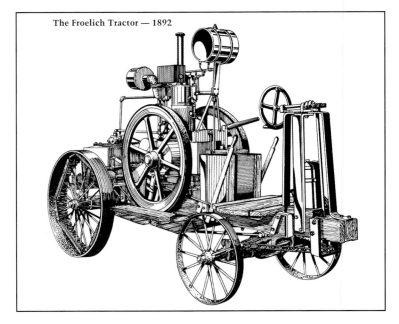

The Froelich Tractor — 1892

Waterloo Gasoline Traction Engine.

16-HORSE POWER.

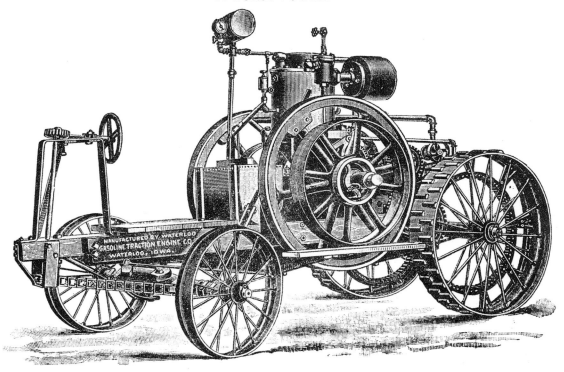

The Froelich engine could deliver at least 16 horsepower, an enormous amount of power for work, which made it worth the effort of maintaining. This sketch shows the improved offset lugs and gives a clear view of Froelich's chain-steering mechanism. *Voyageur Press Archives*

A successful tractor in its day, the Waterloo Boy Model R had a production run that numbered 9,310 units and spanned five years. During that time—on March 14, 1918, to be exact—the Waterloo Gasoline Engine Company became part of the John Deere family. The Model R's engine needed two kinds of fuel: gasoline to get it started and kerosene to keep it running.

An early version of the Waterloo Boy Model R. In this early edition, the kerosene fuel tank was raised on brackets and laid horizontally at the front of the tractor. However, the machine had fuel flow problems on steep hills. Later designs of the Model R lowered the tank and placed it vertically. This view also depicts the radiator, mounted transverse to the axis of the machine and to the direction of airflow. *Voyageur Press Archives*

A chassis drawing of the Waterloo Boy Model R. This view gives a clearer look at the right-side steering mechanism, which translates torque on the steering wheel to chains, shown lying slack on either side of the front axle. Also well depicted is the transmission with its enormous drive gear. *Voyageur Press Archives*

A beautiful romanticized painting of farm life at the turn of the twentieth century adorns the side of this Model R. The boy in this painting is undoubtedly a waterboy—a younger worker whose responsibilities included fetching water for older hands—from whom the Waterloo Boy tractor gets its name.

A closeup look at the gear mesh between the drive gear of the Model N and the tractor's driveshaft. The Model N can be easily distinguished from the earlier Model R by its drive gear, which is almost as large as its rear wheel, with teeth pointed inward to engage the just-visible driveshaft. The teeth on the drive gear of the Model R point outward.

Waterloo Boy Model R	
Engine:	Overhead-valve two-cylinder
Bore & Stroke:	5.50x7.00 inches (styles A–D)
	6.00x7.00 inches (styles E–L)
	6.50x7.00 (style M)
Engine Speed:	750 rpm
Displacement:	465 ci
Power:	25 belt horsepower
Transmission:	One-speed forward
Weight:	6,000 pounds

Waterloo Boy advertisement depicting a stationary Waterloo Boy engine pumping water for farm animals. For farmers at the turn of the twentieth century, the tractor did a much better job providing static power than it did pulling implements. *Voyageur Press Archives*

The text at the bottom of this advertisement describes the Waterloo Boy Model R as a "reliable three plow tractor." It also touts the tractor as having a "plowing record of 18 cents per acre and threshing record of 15 cents per hour on kerosene." *Voyageur Press Archives*

Meets All Power Requirements

Two-Speed
12-25 H. P.
Hyatt
Roller
Bearings
Automatic
Lubrication

WATERLOO BOY
ORIGINAL KEROSENE TRACTOR

Experience has demonstrated that this three-plow tractor, with 25 H.P. at belt is the ideal "general utility" tractor for any size farm. Its light weight, simplicity, great durability, ample power and economy give it

The Widest Range of Availability
At Minimum Operating Cost

Discriminating buyers are choosing the Waterloo Boy because of its demonstrated success in the hands of users under all conditions; because it is built and fully guaranteed by a responsible manufacturer; because of its dependability in emergencies, unusual fuel economy, and because conveniently located distributors insure prompt and courteous service when needed.

Write for free illustrated catalog giving full information.

Geo. W. Brending, Milford, Ill., writes: "Your tractor has given complete satisfaction. I plowed seventy acres in eight days with a three-bottom John Deere Plow; did most of my discing with it using two 18 in. wheel discs at all times. Kept close record of operating cost—$2 per day paid for all fuel and lubricating oil when doing a full day's work."

Chas. W. Carlson, Stromburg, Neb., writes: "Your tractor is O. K. It is cheap to operate—not more than two gallons kerosene to the acre, plowing good depth, with 3-bottom 14 in. John Deere Plow. Plowed old alfalfa, sod pasture, stock and stubble ground without trouble. I use the tractor to pull 28 in. thresher and thresh 33 loads of wheat to a barrel of kerosene."

JOHN DEERE, 1703 W. Third Ave., Moline, Ill.

Another Waterloo Boy advertisement, proclaiming the tractor offers "the widest range of availability at minimum operating cost." *Voyageur Press Archives*

Henry "Harry" George Ferguson, an Irishman, looked to the Waterloo Boy Models R and N to help redeem farm-labor losses in World War I by importing the tractors and distributing them through London. The green tractors were repainted Rumely Green, Allis-Chalmers Orange, and Battleship Gray and were renamed Overtimes. *Randy Leffingwell*

Overtime Model R	
Engine:	Overhead-valve two-cylinder
Bore & Stroke:	6.00x7.00 inches (styles E–L)
	6.50x7.00 (style M and Model N)
Engine Speed:	750 rpm
Displacement:	465 ci
Power:	25 belt horsepower
Transmission:	One-speed forward; Model N:
	Two-speed forward
Weight:	6,000 pounds; Model N: 6,300 pounds

An Overtime in the fields of England. The easily recognized form of a Waterloo Boy tractor is shown working under farmers who look undeterred by the broken wheel on the plow behind them. *Voyageur Press Archives*

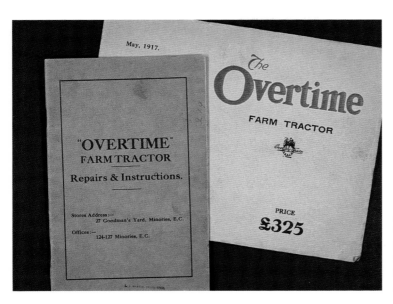

A 1917 Overtime farm tractor brochure, including repair and instructions for use. Note the price of the tractor: £325. *Voyageur Press Archives*

The Two-Cylinder Legends

Five Model As arranged in order of production, from 1934 to 1938. All of these tractors had 5.5x6.5-inch bore-and-stroke engines, burning kerosene or distillate. All told, fourteen variations of the Model A were made by Deere & Company, each designed to meet diverse farming needs based on farm size, geography, and crop.

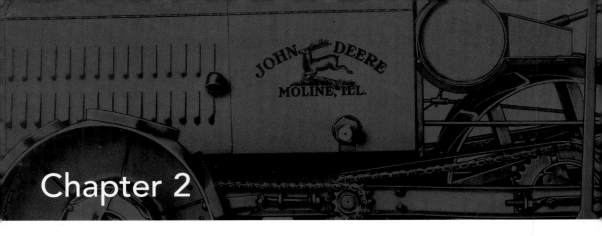

Chapter 2

The tractor industry in the 1920s was still in its infancy. Despite the successes of Henry Ford and the International Harvester Company—and the growing contributions of Deere & Company—many farmers doubted that these new machines were really more efficient than horses and human labor. They could pull harder and longer, and they cost less to maintain, but very few farmers owned one.

In 1931, even as the U.S. Department of Agriculture tallied the one millionth tractor sold, it estimated that only one in six farmers had one. This was due to a variety of factors: The initial investment was considerable, the product was unfamiliar, and much of available tractor machinery was just plain shoddy.

In this market climate, Deere launched its first major production tractor, the Model D, in 1923. It was a two-cylinder machine, reflecting Deere's granite-hard commitment to the design. Deere's head of sales, Frank Silloway, summarized the advantages of two-cylinders over four in a famous memo in 1917, pointing out that two-cylinder tractors were cheaper to build than four and that repairing two-cylinder machines and inventorying them would be easier.

Starting with the Model D and its Waterloo Boy forebears, Deere stayed committed to the two-cylinder design concept for decades to come, making the company almost synonymous with twin-cylinder tractor power until 1960.

With the Model D, Deere was looking to carve out a niche in the upper end of the market. It sold for $1,000 as opposed to Henry Ford's Fordson, a lighter-duty machine, which cost less than half as much. The D was not an overnight success, but by its third year of production, the tractor was turning a profit.

As would become a Deere engineering trademark, model improvements came in the midst of production—in fact, almost immediately. With the 51st Model D produced, the company beefed up the tractor's obvious weak point and changed its front axle from a set of welded pieces to a casting. And when the D's spoked flywheel became a menace to life on the farm, it was replaced with a solid flywheel, less apt to entangle farmers' limbs.

In 1924, in the midst of the D's production run, International Harvester introduced the celebrated Farmall tractor, a truly innovative farm worker that added the easy cultivation of crops to plowing functions. With its tricycle design, the Farmall could pass over two rows of crops without damaging them.

It was a sensation and demanded a response, which came in the form of Deere's Model C. While the C was not a tricycle design, its high-arched front axle allowed crops to pass under during cultivation. But it had a power takeoff, a power lift for implements to be raised and lowered, and newly designed rear brakes, all of which helped to justify the extra $200 it cost over the Farmall.

The Model C was intended as an all-around tractor, but its name was phonetically confusing with the Model D, so it was simply renamed the Model GP, for General Purpose, in 1927.

This tractor's Nebraska test took place on April 19, 1934, in Lincoln. The Model AO's drawbar horsepower rating of 18 (maximum load test) was measured with the drive wheels equipped with spade lugs and extension rims. In the test remarks, observers noted that "we find no claims and statements [in the advertising literature of this tractor] which, in our opinion, are unreasonable or excessive."

But the cultivating tractor market still wanted a powerful tricycle design that could pass two standard-width rows of crops. And that's what it got in 1929 with the Model GPWT (General Purpose Wide Tread). The GPWT was an immediate crowd-pleaser, and it sold 2,039 units by April 1930, and another 3,215 after that before it finished production in 1933.

With these changes in design, the early tractor models, plow pullers such as the Waterloo Boy Model N and the Model D, were diversifying to handle different farm jobs and then crop types. A potato farmer in Maine needed something a little different than a cotton farmer in

Alabama. What was needed in the Pacific Northwest's apple country was a good orchard tractor, which Deere supplied with the Model GPO (General Purpose Orchard) in 1931. This production run started with tractors sporting steel wheels, then hard molded rubber tires, then low-pressure balloon tires, and finally some tractors were fitted with tracks to better suit the orchard environment.

As the Model D and GP were maturing as designs, engineers at Deere were working on two new models to capture the crop farmer market: the Model A and Model B. Launched within months of each other, they offered many of the same innovations, such as optional pneumatic tires and adjustable wheel spacing. The big difference between them was size; the Model B was about two-thirds as big.

Within these base model ranges, Deere offered variations to suit individual needs. Farmers needing the A's powerful engine could get it in a vehicle configuration to fit their crop scheme. The Model AN had narrow tread, ANH was narrow with a high axle, AW was wide, AWH was wide and high, AO was specially adapted for orchards, and so on. Likewise, the more affordable Model B offered these same variations, but in a smaller package.

Late in the decade, Deere added a substantial amount of horsepower to this design with the Model G. The G was very similar to the A and B, but for large operations it added a whopping 50 percent more horsepower.

Starting in 1937, Henry Dreyfuss and his team of industrial engineers took these tractors and tamed them for the market, giving them some style. "Styled" tractors had a makeover, which analyzed and improved the basic model in five areas: utility and safety, ease of maintenance, cost of production, sales appeal, and appearance. Tractors from the years before this transformation became known as "unstyled."

Above and opposite page: Billed as a one-plow tractor, the Model BW had a 149-cubic-inch displacement engine designed to run at 1,150 rpm and produce 11 horsepower at the drawbar, sufficient for its small-farm customers. *Andy Kraushaar/Hans Halberstadt*

The John Deere Model D Spoker came equipped with a 6.5x7.0-inch bore-and-stroke kerosene engine; a large, molded seat; and deep lugs on its iron wheels. Built early in the production run, this edition was fitted with a 24-inch spoked flywheel. With its enormous weight spinning at high rpm, the open flywheel proved to be a severe hazard for farmers—anything caught in it would be mangled.

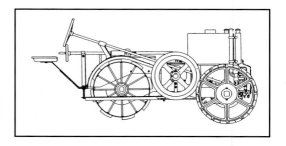

Model D 1923–1925	
Engine:	Overhead-valve two-cylinder
Bore & Stroke:	6.50x7.00 inches
Engine Speed:	800 rpm
Displacement:	482 ci
Power:	27 belt horsepower
Transmission:	Two-speed forward
Weight:	4,000 pounds

Very early schematic for the Model D. By the time this tractor rolled down the assembly line, a number of changes had been made to this design, including the altering radius of the front wheels. *Voyageur Press Archives*

A 1923 Model D Spoker, so named for its 24-inch diameter, six-spoked flywheel. Soon after this tractor was made in 1925, Model Ds changed to solid flywheels keyed to the crankshaft.

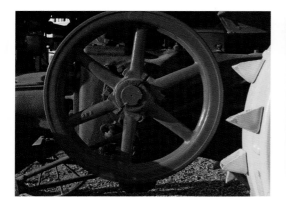

Going for a ride on a Model D Spoker. Accentuated high against the sky are its conspicuous air intake and exhaust. Also visible here is one of Deere's Model D flywheel redesigns. This one would be scrapped, too, after reports that it often cracked in the field.

The fenders, seat, floor, and wheel of a 1923 Model D Spoker. The iron seat shown here was manufactured at a time when comfort was lower on Deere's design priority list. It wasn't until 1937 that Henry Dreyfuss addressed the problem of sore bottoms with a more ergonomic seat.

The steel wheels featured on this 1925 Model D Spoker soon became old news on American farms as tractors sporting pneumatic tires became the norm. Some historians believe that the most important tractor innovation was the change from steel wheels—which tore up ground, jarred the farmer terribly, slipped easily (despite the lugs), slowed the tractor, and restricted it from roads—to pneumatic tires.

Model D Two-Speed 1926–1933	
Engine:	Overhead-valve two-cylinder
Bore & Stroke:	6.75x7.00 inches
Engine Speed:	900 rpm
Displacement:	501 ci
Power:	47 horsepower
Transmission:	Two-speed forward
Weight:	4,822 pounds

Model D Three-Speed 1934–1939	
Engine:	Overhead-valve two-cylinder
Bore & Stroke:	6.75x7.00 inches
Engine speed:	900 rpm
Displacement:	501 ci
Power:	42 horsepower
Transmission:	Three-speed forward
Weight:	5,300 pounds

Model D Spoker with cast front axle, a dramatic improvement over its previous welded axle. This model has offset lugs on its rear wheels, another attempt to deal with the traction problems that persisted with earlier-design steel rear wheels.

A 1930 Model D is shown here pulling a power binder, an excellent example of how tractor power led to the invention of dozens of new labor-saving, production-multiplying machines on the farm. The result was an explosion of farm yields. *Voyageur Press Archives*

Model D advertisement depicting the most important function of tractors of the period: pulling a plow. Tractor functionality would be expanded dramatically with attachments and implements of all kinds in later years. *Voyageur Press Archives*

Brochure touting the virtues of the Model D, specifically its power and capability for large farm jobs. The tractor shown here uses its belt pulley to power a thresher, one of many power applications of its 30-horsepower kerosene (gasoline start) engine. *Voyageur Press Archives*

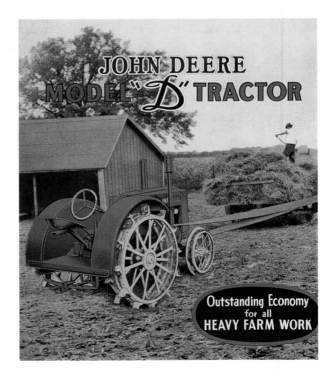

This 1924 calendar image shows a youngster driving his Model D with a No. 5 plow and waving to an airplane and its pilot. *Voyageur Press Archives*

A 1928 version of a John Deere Model C tractor. This was an early attempt to design a machine that could cultivate growing plants, as is evident in its high-clearance front axle, wider tread arrangement, and more nimble look.

Model C 1926–1927	
Engine:	Two-cylinder L-head
Bore & Stroke:	5.75x6.00 inches
Engine Speed:	950 rpm
Displacement:	312 ci
Power:	20 horsepower
Transmission:	Three-speed forward
Weight:	3,600 pounds

This Model C, built in 1928, provides an interesting comparison to the previous photo. The front axle is arched, but narrower, and it sports the double-wide rear wheels with offset lugs. It also has an updated solid flywheel with stress-relief slots capped by larger-diameter openings.

This Model C demonstrates exactly what is meant by the phrase "two-plow tractor." It was a valuable asset for farmers in the late 1920s and 1930s, partly due to its versatility. It delivered power from its drawbar, PTO, mechanical power lift, and a belt pulley. With a bit of ingenuity, these features could be applied to tackle a variety of farm jobs. *Voyageur Press Archives*

JOHN DEERE
MOLINE, ILL.

Originally the Model C, this tractor's moniker was switched to "GP" (General Purpose) to avoid the possibility of confusion between the like-sounding C and D models over crackling phone lines in the late 1920s. In the run-up to production in 1928, the GP's tooling at the Waterloo factory cost a heady $3.9 million, but it more than paid for itself in the long term, ultimately selling over 30,000 units at a 1931 asking price of $1,200.

The Model GP (General Purpose) incorporated several innovations from the engineers at Deere & Company. It had an arched front axle for better clearance directly under the centerline of the tractor (important for cultivation and passing obstructions), and it also had a PTO. Early versions of the GP had iron wheels, but by 1929, when this tractor was born, some were outfitted with rubber tires.

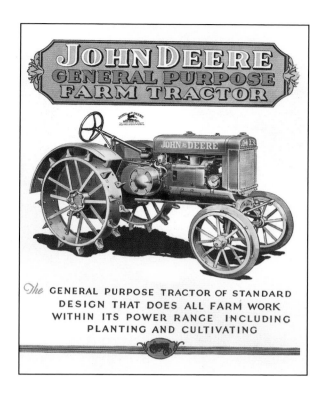

Model GP tractor advertisement stressing the evolution of Deere tractors from simple plowing machines to a tool that could do "all farm work within its power range, including planting and cultivating." *Voyageur Press Archives*

A pristine condition 1929 Model GP outfitted with pneumatic tires and its owner J. Wilke. At its Nebraska test, the GP put out 25.36 horsepower at its belt pulley and PTO, and precisely half that at its drawbar, an unusually low ratio. It ran on kerosene, but needed gasoline to get started.

Model GP (styles 1 and 2) 1928–1930	
Engine:	Two-cylinder L-head
Bore & Stroke:	5.75x6.00 inches
Engine Speed:	950 rpm
Displacement:	312 ci
Power:	20 horsepower
Transmission:	Three-speed forward
Weight:	3,600 pounds

By 1931, when this tractor was made, the GP had dramatically improved its pulling ability. With a new, bigger-bore engine, the later model GP had raised drawbar horsepower by 50 percent and was running on distillate fuel.

A 1931 Model GP shown in evening light. Later versions of the GP such as this one featured an improved air cleaner and intake stack on the left side of the hood. Earlier editions had air intake louvers between the cylinder and radiator, or a vertical intake stack on the right side, as on the 1929 Model GP.

An early Model GP with corn row planter. Along with cultivation and plowing, planting was a farm job Deere wanted to bring onto its résumé. This Model 301 three-row planter remains an attractive accessory to the GP, but it never caught on in the market.

In 1935, when this Model GP came off the assembly line, the tractor was in its final year of production. Yet it was still receiving updates, such as this machine's Vortox air cleaner, which used an oil bath to trap air-borne particles.

Model GP (styles 3, 4, 5) 1930–1935	
Engine:	Two-cylinder L-head
Bore & Stroke:	6.00x6.00 inches
Engine Speed:	950 rpm
Displacement:	339 ci
Power:	25 horsepower
Transmission:	Three-speed forward
Weight:	3,600 pounds

The final production tally on the GP in 1935 was 30,754 tractors, establishing it as a solid bridge from the Model C to the great row-crop tractors, the Models A and B, already ramping up production.

By 1935 farmers could have pneumatic tires either as original equipment or retrofitted, and the tires were, in most respects, far superior to steel. Still, in some soil conditions, lugs such as these offered better traction.

JOHN DEERE
MOLINE, ILL.

This 1931 version of the popular GP tractor, which offered a wide stance in the back, was given the designation GPWT, for "General Purpose Wide Tread." It could straddle two rows of crops with its 44x10-inch rear wheels and split them with its 24-inch double front wheels.

Like the GP, the GPWT had a power lift feature that was quite endearing to farmers, particularly those who were less physically capable.

The GPWT had three gears forward and one reverse, and it was capable of reaching four miles per hour, or just about walking speed, with the throttle wide open.

In Deere's alphabetical tractor-designation system, GPO stood for "General Purpose Orchard." This early Model GPO, built in 1931, had modifications like solid front wheels (in which branches would not be caught) and sloping fenders. These made it more productive on fruit farms.

Right: Note the absence of an exhaust or intake stack on this 1931 Model GPO. The overall height of this tractor was reduced to an amazing 49 inches (to the radiator cap, 51 inches to the top arch of the fenders) for better clearance under trees.

Opposite page: Built for a specialty market, only 589 GPOs rolled off the production line at the Waterloo factory. The tractor sold for $855.

This Model A, built in 1934, was one of the first of a line that would run for 18 years and span approximately 300,000 units. Over that time, Deere incorporated many upgrades into the Model A, but its description remained the same; it was a heavy-duty row-crop tractor made for large-scale farming.

With pneumatic tires, the Model A was capable of 6.25 miles per hour and a maximum pull of 2,923 pounds. As an option, it came equipped with a Delco-Remy six-volt electric start system and lighting equipment with a belt-driven generator.

An advertisement for the new Model A and B Series with farm boy driver. Both the A and B had an I-shaped head and ran on distillate fuel. The Model A popped along at 975 rated rpm, with a compression ratio just shy of 4:1.
Voyageur Press Archives

Model A Series 1932–1934

Engine:	Overhead-valve two-cylinder
Bore & Stroke:	5.50x6.50 inches
Engine Speed:	975 rpm
Displacement:	309 ci
Power:	25 horsepower
Transmission:	Four-speed forward
Weight:	3,675 pounds

A 1934 Model A armed with skeleton steel wheels. In its first production year, 1934, the Model A had a 5.5x6.5-inch bore-and-stroke engine that produced 18.72 horsepower at the drawbar.

Above: By 1943, the Model A had undergone significant changes from the previous decade. Its larger, higher compression engine was developing 34.14 horsepower at the drawbar and could pull more than 4,000 pounds. A six-volt or 12-volt Delco-Remy starter became standard, and its six-speed transmission could make 12 miles per hour between the fields.

Below: A 1937 Model A fitted with skeleton wheels and rigged with a tiller. Note the alignment of wheels on the tractor and the tiller. *Voyageur Press Archives*

Almost ungainly in its appearance, the Model AWH (A Wide High) satisfied farmers who wanted extra clearance in a wide row-crop tractor. This tractor featured a standard Fairbanks-Morse magneto ignition and optional extension rims in the front and rear.

As can be seen here, farmers in the late 1930s still endured a day of plowing and cultivating sitting on a curved piece of iron with ventilation holes.

Like all the Model As, the AWH could burn a variety of fuels, including distillate, fuel oil, furnace oil, and other relatively cheap fuels. The two huge cylinders of the John Deere tractors did this more effectively than competing four- and six-cylinder tractors. It was a competitive edge during the Depression years of the 1930s, and on into the 1940s when gasoline was rationed and alternative fuels were often the only ones available.

JOHN DEERE

MOLINE, ILL.

Right: A gleaming Model AR (A Regular), the final version, built in 1952. In its last year of production, a Model A could be purchased for about $2,500.

Below: After 18 years of innovations and design changes, a host of popular features were standard equipment on the Model AR (some of which can be seen in these photographs), including a hydraulic power lift, an adjustable cushioned seat, front and rear lights, an adjustable swinging drawbar, and electric start.

The AR did not have the flexibility of the other Model As—with their adjustable wheel tread— but offered a robust fixed-tread machine for grass and grain farmers. The final versions of the AR were styled (as is evident here) and had six-speed transmissions.

JOHN DEERE
MOLINE, ILL.

Launched almost concurrently with the Model A, the B was essentially a two-thirds-scale model of the A. Like its heavier, stronger brother, it offered a slew of attractive features, such as a five-speed transmission and steel or pneumatic rubber tires, adjustable wheel spacing to fit the individual farmer's crop scheme, hydraulics, and individual wheel braking.

In 1940, three years after this tractor was manufactured, a regular Model B tractor sold for $715 with steel wheels and $875 with spoked wheels. Ultimately, in all its variations, the Model B sold more tractors than any other two-cylinder tractor, even the Model A.

Model B Series 1934–1938	
Engine:	Overhead-valve two-cylinder
Bore & Stroke:	4.25x5.25 inches
Engine Speed:	1,150 rpm
Displacement:	149 ci
Power:	16 horsepower
Transmission:	Four-speed forward
Weight:	2,731 pounds

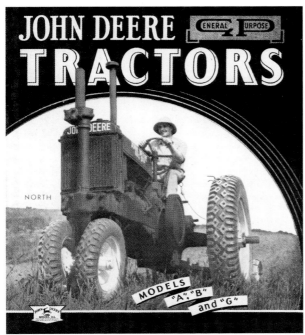

Dubbed a "garden tractor," this variant of the Model B had a single 22.5x8-inch front tire. Note the arched yoke holding the front tire in place and its completely external linkage over the radiator, across the hood to the steering wheel.

A brochure advertising the Model A, B, and G, under the heading of general purpose tractors. With these models, Deere cemented its reputation as a comprehensive farming equipment manufacturer. *Voyageur Press Archives*

JOHN DEERE
MOLINE, ILL.

This unstyled 1937 Model BW tractor has a spiderlike appearance, but for the right farming operation, it was the perfect tractor with its 56- to 80-inch range of adjustment in tread width.

A closeup shot of a 1937 Model BW adjustable rear wheel. The BW was a solid performer, but its market was limited, and only 246 were ever produced. It started up using gas and a Fairbanks Morse magneto, and then ran on distillate.

A total of 1,001 Model BN tractors were built, including this Model BNH (H for high), the eight-bolt pedestal version, of which 977 were made. The BNH was intended for growers of tall vegetable crops. In 1938, this version was followed by the BWH.

Only 24 garden tractors were manufactured with the four-bolt pedestal design shown here, the first of which was completed October 17, 1934, and shipped to Phoenix, Arizona.

The John Deere Model AO was a successful orchard tractor from the moment it was launched in 1934. It was based almost entirely on the Model AR, with a 5.5x6.5-inch bore-and-stroke engine and a four-speed transmission. All protruding components have been streamlined to prevent branches and brush from either striking or becoming lodged in the crevices of the tractor.

The Model AO's 309-cubic-inch engine produced 18 horsepower at the drawbar and 24 horsepower at the PTO and belt during Nebraska tests. It had a rated rpm of 975, a compression ratio of 4.45:1, and it could burn a variety of fuels.

The 1935 Model BO was a smaller version of the Model AO, with distinctive styling on the fenders, radiator cap, and hood. It had a 4.25x5.25-inch bore-and-stroke engine rated at 1,150 rpm. In its initial year of production, the Model BO produced a maximum belt horsepower of 16.01 and a drawbar horsepower of 11.84. *Hans Halberstadt*

The transmission on the 1935 Model BO drove four-foot-diameter rear wheels and was engaged with a disc hand clutch. In top gear, it could reach 6.75 miles per hour forward and 3.50 in reverse. According to its Nebraska test report, still on file in the archives at the University of Nebraska in Lincoln, the Model BO took four gallons of SAE 30 weight oil at the start of its 75-hour test, and at the end 2.65 gallons were drained. *Hans Halberstadt*

JOHN DEERE

MOLINE, ILL.

Right: This 1947 John Deere Model BO Lindeman traces its roots to the early 1930s, when an innovative Deere dealer from Washington, Jesse Lindeman, took it upon himself to put tracks on a John Deere GP tractor. As a testament to this inventor, the tractor bears his name.

Below: With the extra traction provided by tracks and a front blade, this 1946 Model BO Lindeman tractor becomes an effective tool for a variety of pushing jobs. It was a specialist, of course, and only about 3,500 units were made.

The Model BO Lindeman was slightly narrower than the regular edition of the Model B, which helped it slip between the rows of fruit trees. Its low profile and super grip in loose soil made it an ideal orchard tractor.

The Model G, which began production in the middle of Deere & Company's centennial year, 1937, filled out Deere's general purpose tractor line, with one- (Model B), two- (Model A), and three-plow (Model G) tractors.

The Model G had an all-fuel engine after 1941, although conversion kits were available that could convert the tractor to run on gasoline, which was said to improve belt horsepower to 50 horse-power from the measured 38.10 horsepower.

This Model G, with its 412-cubic-inch engine, was built in 1942. Later that year, on September 21, 1942, production of the Model G stopped due to the United States' reorganization of industry, brought on by World War II. Production of the Model G resumed over two years later, on October 16, 1944, with the next serial number machine.

Model G 1937–1941

Engine:	Overhead-valve two-cylinder
Bore & Stroke:	6.125x7.00 inches
Engine Speed:	975 rpm
Displacement:	412.5 ci
Power:	35.9 horsepower
Transmission:	Four-speed forward
Weight:	4,400 pounds

Making Machines with Style

The first effects of Henry Dreyfuss' makeover to John Deere tractors are evident in the rock-ribbed industrial grille and smoothed lines of this 1939 styled Model B. With some mechanical improvements over the initial Model B, which was launched in 1935, this tractor was up to 14.93 horsepower at the drawbar and 18.53 at the belt.

Chapter 3

By the mid-1930s, Deere & Company had established a reputation for producing reliable tractors with ample power. Upgrades to the Model D had turned it into a tool that farmers could count on, and the Models A and B offered solid, general purpose one- and two-plow options.

Still, despite practical functionality, the Deere lineup had a slightly ungainly look to it. The lines on the machines often came together at jarring angles, and components were placed awkwardly, often interfering with sight lines or making them inaccessible for repair. The tractors' seats were slightly curved pieces of iron. Even for the farm beasts of burden they were, they lacked grace, especially compared with the sleek modern machines that the rest of the world was producing. Trains, buildings, and automobiles of the era had taken on a polished demeanor, and Deere's tractors appeared outdated.

The man who would change all that—Henry Dreyfuss, an accomplished industrial designer—lived in New York and had never even heard of John Deere until he was approached by Deere Vice President Elmer McCormick. A typical plainsman, McCormick got right to the point. "We'd like your help in making our tractors more salable," he said. That was the essence of the Deere industrial design movement.

Dreyfuss agreed, moved to the Midwest, and got to work cleaning up the designs of Deere tractors. As stated on his office lobby wall, his goal was to improve design in the following ways:

* Utility and safety
* Ease of maintenance
* Cost of production
* Sales appeal and
* Appearance.

From that day forward, a tractor that had been redesigned, smoothed, and polished by Dreyfuss or his colleagues would be known as a "styled" tractor. Those that had not would be known as "unstyled." The word is misleading, however, because these redesigns imparted a good deal more than just "style." First up for a makeover were Models A and B. The tractors were given bold new lines and an enclosed steering wheel, and the radiator was pulled in behind a muscular new grille—changes that improved appearance and operator visibility.

The big orchard tractor, Model AO, was given a tree-friendly streamlined body with a V-shaped radiator grille and guards to keep tree limbs out. The exhaust stack was taken off and vented to the side.

The Model L, an awkward-looking tractor if one were ever made, was given the full Dreyfuss treatment. Its edges were smoothed and curved, its parts pulled in and integrated, and the engine was upgraded. By the time it emerged in 1939, it was a different machine. And for the first time in company history, Deere simply stopped making the older version and began rolling out the new.

Launched at the same time as the Model L were Models G and H, which fit neatly into different segments of the Deere lineup. The H dovetailed into a gap between mid-sized and small row croppers, and the G was the company's first three-plow tractor. Both would eventually be given Deere's new, highly marketable industrial look with rock-ribbed grilles and smooth, flush surfaces.

In 1946, Deere's facilities expanded to a new factory in Dubuque, Iowa, and the first tractor to roll through the newly opened doors was the gasoline-driven Model M. By this time, styling was not restricted to redesign; the Dreyfuss principles of appearance and form were standard operating procedure for all tractors, new and upgrades. The well-packed Model M was issued in a crawler version, the MC, and an adjustable track width Model MT.

By the late 1940s the Henry Dreyfuss look was well established in Deere marketing, and it was clear that farmers felt more comfortable on styled tractors, and most preferred them. While the precise look of the styling changed over the years, the principles of Henry Dreyfuss' industrial design remained.

Tractors became refined in the mid-1930s after streamlined styles of automobiles, trains, and buildings had already caught the attention of the public.

A styled Model D posed in a half-plowed field. In 1948, when this tractor was built, the Model D was nearing the end of its incredible production run, which was longer than any other piece of John Deere equipment. The first Model D rolled off the assembly line in March 1923, and the last Model D built in July 1953.

Model D 1939–1946

Engine:	Overhead-valve two-cylinder
Bore & Stroke:	6.75x7.00 inches
Engine Speed:	900 rpm
Displacement:	501 ci
Power:	42 horsepower
Transmission:	Three-speed forward
Weight:	5,300 pounds

This view displays some of the Model D's styled elements, including its optional electric lights. By 1948, the Model D had come a long way from its steel-wheeled, 15-drawbar horsepower, two-speed transmission origins. This model could boast 28.53 drawbar horsepower, 36.98 horsepower at the belt, and a 5.25-mile-per-hour top speed.

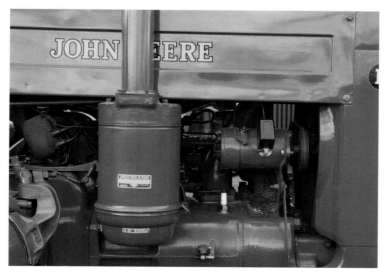

A closeup of the Model D's Donaldson oil bath air cleaner, which used an oil-soaked filter medium to trap dust before it could enter the engine and cause damage. Donaldson Equipment, Inc., of St. Paul, Minnesota, began as a vendor to Deere & Company during the 1920s and became a major supplier in the following decades. The sticker on the air cleaner reads: "Service every 30 hours when frequently under severe dust conditions."

JOHN DEERE
MOLINE, ILL.

This styled version of the Model A enclosed the radiator behind the grille and featured a solid rear wheel as opposed to the earlier spoked Model A. Also, the steering shaft, which had run the length of the tractor and over the top of the radiator, was now smoothly enclosed within the hood, just to the right of the centerline.

Model A Series 1938–1952

Engine:	Overhead-valve two-cylinder
Bore & Stroke:	5.50x6.75 inches
Engine Speed:	975 rpm
Displacement:	321 ci
Power:	29.59 horsepower
Transmission:	Four-speed forward early; six-speed forward late
Weight:	3,817 pounds

Right: In 1941, starting with serial number 499000, the transmission was changed from four forward speeds to six. Like earlier versions, this 1944 Model A ran on distillate, using 3.3 gallons of SAE 30 weight oil.

Opposite page: An overhead shot of a 1943 Model A. This tractor used an oil-washed, crimped wire air cleaner from the United Company and a Purolator oil filter. It had six-ply, 38-inch rear tires inflated to 16 psi and four-ply, 16-inch front tires inflated to 28 psi.

By 1952, style changes on the Model A had reached full development. The padded seat had replaced the earlier Model A's pressed steel, headlights were in place, and the air intake and exhaust were shorter, of larger diameter, and parallel to the centerline of the machine instead of side by side.

An open fan shaft on a Model A styled tractor. A portion of the fan shafts on Model A tractors—from serial number 414809 to 424024—was exposed between the upper water pipe and the governor housing, making these tractors relatively rare and collectible Model As.

A styled Model A sits on the left, and an unstyled Model A on the right. Just on the surface, many design changes are apparent, from lights to gauges to seating to sheet metal, but they can be summed up in the styled A's cleaner, more modern look.

As can be seen in this photograph, the front axle width on this late-styled 1949 Model BW (sometimes called an "anteater nose") was adjustable; it could be set anywhere between 56 to 80 inches. Although the Model B was a brilliant success overall, selling more tractors than any other two-cylinder model, the BW variant was not. Its production run ended at 246 units.

Model B Series 1938–1958	
Engine:	Overhead-valve two-cylinder
Bore & Stroke:	4.50x5.50 inches early;
	4.69x5.50 inches late
Engine Speed:	1,150 rpm early; 1,250 late
Displacement:	175 ci early; 1,250 late
Power:	18.53 horsepower early;
	23.53 horsepower late
Transmission:	Six-speed forward
Weight:	2,763 pounds

In terms of power and weight, this Model B was roughly two-thirds the size of the concurrently introduced Model A and gave small-tractor customers a Deere option. *Voyageur Press Archives*

This Model B, baling hay in the midday sun, can be identified as a styled model by its integrated steering shaft, solid rear wheels, and enclosed grille. *Voyageur Press Archives*

Model G Series 1942–1953	
Engine:	Overhead-valve two-cylinder
Bore & Stroke:	6.125x7.00 inches
Engine Speed:	975 rpm
Displacement:	412.5 ci
Power:	38.10 horsepower
Transmission:	Six-speed forward
Weight:	5,100 pounds

The Model G was originally to be designated Model F, but International Harvester had already hit the market with its Farmall F and Deere wanted a clear distinction between the two. A host of design improvements distinguished this later-styled 1950 Model G from its earlier incarnations, including its cushy seat and solid rear wheels. The original G also had a smaller radiator, but its cooling capacity proved insufficient, so it was replaced with a larger unit.

This 1953 Model GW had an adjustable front-tread width and internal expansion brakes located on independent shafts geared to each rear axle, operated by one foot pedal on each side. These could be locked simply by latching them to the tractor platform.

The Model G had an "all-fuel" engine after 1941 and recorded a belt horsepower of 38.10 and drawbar horsepower of 34.49 in Nebraska tests. Its 6.125x7-inch bore-and-stroke engine was rated at 975 rpm.

Sitting high off the ground, the Model G High-Crop was a powerful tractor built to pass over tall rows. It had cast-iron rear wheels (fitted with 12x38 six-ply tires, inflated to 14 psi) that weighed a total of 670 pounds. Its front steel disc wheel weighed just 30 pounds, and it used four-ply tires inflated to 28 psi.

At full throttle, this 1952 Model G High-Crop consumed nearly four gallons of fuel per hour and operated at 198 degrees Fahrenheit. At its rated load, its fuel consumption dropped to 2.8 gallons per hour, giving the tractor about six hours in the field before refueling its 17-gallon tank.

This 1952 Model G High-Crop could manage a brisk 12.5-mile-per-hour speed on the road in high gear. It had a Purolator full-flow filter and a Donaldson oil-washed wire-screen air cleaner.

A gleaming 1944 Model H tractor. Introduced just before the onset of World War II in 1939, the Model H was a small to midsize row-crop tractor capable of 32 inches of adjustment in rear tread width. It filled the space in the Deere lineup between the compact Model L and the larger Model B.

An interesting feature on the Model H design is the use of the camshaft instead of the crankshaft to drive the belt pulley and a governor override, which enabled the tractor to reach higher speeds on roads and farm races.

The Model H at work in the field. It used a thrifty 1.3 gallons per hour at 100 percent maximum load and ran at the unusual speed of 1,400 rpm, with an operating temperature of 201 degrees Fahrenheit. *Voyageur Press Archives*

A closeup look at the nose of a 1944 Model H, showing wire screening over its radiator and air intake hole. With over 60,000 units produced between 1939 and 1947 at the Waterloo factory, the Model H was a notable success, partially due to its reasonable price. In 1944, a Model H sold for $641.

Model H Series 1938–1946	
Engine:	Overhead-valve two-cylinder
Bore & Stroke:	3.56x5.00 inches
Engine Speed:	1,400 rpm
Displacement:	90.7 ci
Power:	14.84 horsepower
Transmission:	Three-speed forward
Weight:	2,054 pounds

JOHN DEER
MOLINE, ILL.

The distinguishing feature on this Model HN, built in 1940, is its single front wheel as opposed to the double front wheel on the other Model H variants. It ran on distillate fuel after starting on gas, a feature that served it well during the gas-rationing years of World War II. It was rated at 12.48 horsepower at the drawbar and had a compression ratio of 4.75:1.

A specialty tractor, the John Deere Model HWH (W for wide-front end, H for high-rear end) was given its extra rear clearance by replacing the standard 32-inch Model H rear wheel with a 38-inch Model B wheel.
Hans Halberstadt

Just 126 Model HWH tractors were built by Deere.

The Model L was a lightweight, economical tractor, marketed to the considerable number of small farmers still using horses or mules in the late 1930s for farm work. About 12,500 were built at the Moline plant in Illinois. The Model L sold for $516.75 in 1946. The 9.06-drawbar horsepower Model L was not exceedingly powerful, but it was simple, dependable, and, most important, easily adaptable to a variety of farm jobs.

Late in 1937 the Model L tractor emerged from the John Deere factory in Moline, Illinois, as a replacement for the Model 62. Early models of this tractor were built around an outsourced, two-cylinder Hercules engine. Later, Deere used an engine of its own design. Early models could manage seven horsepower at the drawbar and nine horsepower at the belt.

An advertisement for the Model L. It was a light, thrifty tractor aimed at the considerable number of farmers still using horses. *Voyageur Press Archives*

The Model L at work. Aiding the operation of the Model L was its innovative foot clutch, which replaced the hand clutch. The Model L was powered by a vertical two-cylinder engine instead of a horizontal one. *Voyageur Press Archives*

JOHN DEERE
MOLINE, ILL.

With its individual rear brakes, the Model L had an unusually tight turning radius, which came in handy at the end of the crop row on a small farm. It was the first John Deere tractor on which rubber tires came standard.

A 1945 Model LI, the industrial version of the John Deere Model L. Around 2,500 LIs were built from 1938 to 1946, in three types: unstyled, of which about 70 were made; styled—with a Hercules engine—of which approximately 434 were made; and styled, with a John Deere engine, of which 2,019 were made.

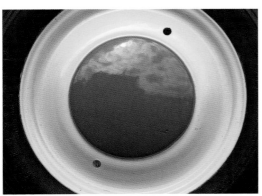

Larger than the Model L, the Model LA was introduced in 1941 and given a 540-rpm PTO and a larger volume engine, which offered a nice boost in power. It also offered the convenient option of an electric starter and lights.

The Model M was designed for smaller-scale farming operations and aimed at customers of Henry Ford's N Series tractors. It had a gas or all-fuel engine capable of 18.15 horsepower at the drawbar and a four-speed transmission capable of 12 miles per hour. In production from 1947 to 1952, it was the first tractor made at Deere's new Dubuque, Iowa, factory.

Model M Series 1947–1955	
Engine:	two-cylinder vertical
Bore & Stroke:	4.00x4.00 inches
Engine Speed:	1,650 rpm
Displacement:	100.5 ci
Power:	20.45 horsepower
Transmission:	Four-speed forward
Weight:	2,560 pounds

This 1948 Model M was a general-purpose utility tractor with vertical cylinder alignment instead of the traditional horizontal arrangement. In all, more than 87,000 Model Ms were produced with production ending in 1952.

Learning from the success of the Model BO Lindeman Crawlers, and after purchasing the Lindeman Power Equipment Company in December 1946, Deere launched the MC Crawler out of its Yakima Works in 1949. In 1954, production was transferred to Deere's Dubuque Tractor Works.

In most respects, this Model MT tractor was the same as the Model M, but it had some handy options on the front axle. It could be specified with different front end arrangements: adjustable wide front, dual-tricycle front, or single-front wheel. It also could be ordered with Touch-O-Matic hydraulic controls.

Based on the Model A, the Model AI offered 18 horsepower for work in a variety of construction and materials handling operations. A solid machine in its niche, the Model AI was built from 1936 to 1941.

Industrial Strength

Chapter 4

Almost as soon as Johnny Popper had proven a dependable hand around the farm, Deere & Company decided to expand the use of its tractors to a new set of applications with the advent of industrial versions of its popular tractor models.

Of course, ever since tractors had been invented, they had been used for a wide variety of purposes beyond nominal farm work, including those that could be considered industrial.

The first Deere machine to be modified for the industrial market was the Model D in 1925. With its steel wheels and lugs, the Model D could handle certain applications, such as pulling a scraper or pushing a grader moldboard in soft soils, but its lugs would tear up any improved road surface. It also needed a bit more flat-out speed in solid conditions.

Although pneumatic tires were not available at the time, Deere outfitted the industrial Model D with hard rubber tires, better speed capability, and lights for working at night.

By 1927, Model Ds had been modified with moldboards to become motor graders. These versions were given much larger fuel tanks to keep them in operation over greater distances, with hard rubber tires and with other changes consistent with carrying a large iron blade.

Such modified machines were produced for various customers for the next decade, but the first industrial tractor to receive official designation was the Model DI, which went into production in 1935.

This move was really the result of a negotiated deal with the Caterpillar Company of Peoria, Illinois. At the time, the companies' dealer networks overlapped in some places, but there were many locations that had either Cat or Deere dealers. So working together would, in effect, give both companies greater dealer coverage. At the same time, Caterpillar needed a wheeled tractor to satisfy some of its industrial product customers. The Deere industrial tractors would do just that.

The Model DI differed from the standard Model D in a number of important respects, and these changes were typical of all the industrialized models. The industrial version of the D had turning brakes and a lever that enabled them to be locked—critical for many construction jobs. The drawbar of the agricultural D was replaced with a heavier, Y-shaped piece of iron more suited to its new application. The transmission was changed to enable the DI to reach a swifter top speed of over seven miles per hour. And finally, the standard pressed iron seat was replaced with a much more comfortable padded one. (Clearly, Deere designers felt that 10 hours of pulling a scraper were a lot harder on the rump than a like period of plowing.)

After the Model DI, Models A and B were given industrial makeovers, and the LI joined the line of industrial machines in 1938. While their agricultural counterparts had been wildly successful, the industrial versions could not come close, and in 1941, as World War II drew near, Deere shut down production of industrial models.

The move was only temporary, however. In 1950, the Deere industrial line was revived with the launch of the Model MI, a version of the high- ly successful and extremely versatile Model M, which had begun production three years earlier out of Deere's new factory in Dubuque, Iowa.

The industrial line of John Deere tractors came about in part because of an unlikely ally: the Caterpillar Company. The two companies decided to collaborate and offer certain prod- ucts from each one at their dealer locations, thus broadening their potential customer base through greater dealer coverage. The Deere industrial tractors were designed to meet the needs of some of Cat's customers.

The Model DI used the same 501-cubic-inch displacement, 6.75x7-inch bore-and-stroke engine rated at 900 rpm as the standard Model D. It started using gasoline from its 1.5-gallon auxiliary fuel tank and ran on kerosene.

The industrial D had heavier rear-axle housings and its brake drums were cast into the rear wheels to better deal with the demands of construction applications. The tractor stood 61.25 inches tall and weighed 5,269 pounds.

The transmission was altered on some Model DIs to give them better speed on good surfaces, although some versions were given lower gearing for even more pulling strength.

The Model AI was based on the Model A with some modifications, often to suit an individual buyer. On this particular tractor, an aftermarket cab and headlights were added to the base unit. It also has fenders and a platform floor with a hole in it to accommodate the lever that operated the Model AI's wheel brakes.

Like all industrial models, Model AIs were modified in different ways for special applications. This 1939 version uses the AI's 5.5x6.5-inch bore-and-stroke engine to power a crane. Essentially an early model forklift, this tractor would have been a valuable asset in this freight yard. Its engine could put out 29 horsepower at the drawbar.

In 1939, electric start and lights became a factory-installed option on Model AIs.

Model AI at work in a contemporary urban setting. The first Model AI was built in April 1936 and the last was built in June 1941.

Like the AI, this 1938 Model BI was given a beefier rear axle, housings, and bearings than its standard version (in this case, the Model B) to handle industrial applications. In addition, the exhaust stack was removed, similar to the Model BO.

This photo of a red Model BI, built in 1937, displays its unique paint job as well as its padded-base, iron back seat, and a hand lever to control its wheel brakes.

A wire screen radiator cover for a red 1937 John Deere Model BI. Deere's industrial tractors were painted a variety of colors over the years, from a hue called Burnt Orange to one known as Special Yellow.

This Model MI differed from its base Model M in a number of ways. It was noticeably lower, and the rear wheels were moved slightly forward. Its drawbar was also given a new design. Notice the change to the fenders, which are flatter and missing the supporting ribs.

In fourth gear, with its 1,650-rpm 4x4-inch bore-and-stroke engine at full throttle, the Model MI could reach 10 miles per hour. In 1952, its final year of production, a John Deere Model MI, with special 6x16-inch, four-ply tires on the front and 10x24-inch, four-ply tires on the rear, sold for $1,379.

Among the optional features on the Model MI were lights, an adjustable front axle, orchard muffler, wheel weights, and an hour meter. These industrial tractors usually were painted Highway Yellow at the factory, but some were coated in Highway Orange.

Deere's Power Players

The Model R owns the distinction of being John Deere's first diesel tractor. Pictured here is a 1952 version in a pastoral setting, shot from an angle that emphasizes the geometric look of tractors of that period, including this tractor's stark rectangular frame and circular flywheel housing and wheels.

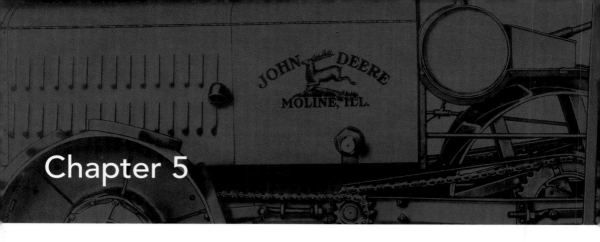

Chapter 5

The 1950s were transition years for Deere & Company. The company had been in the tractor business for over three decades, and in that time, it had not wavered in its loyalty to the non-diesel-fueled, two-cylinder engine concept.

That strategy had worked to a large extent. Deere's tractors were popular for their dependability and maintenance simplicity—just as Frank Silloway had foreseen in his memo of 1917 when he outlined the advantages of a simple, basic design.

But in the post–World War II years, the needs of farmers began to change. Labor was more expensive and scarce. Farms were larger, and what they needed more than ever before were higher horsepower tractors with plenty of torque for ripping ever-larger plows through the soil. This would lead to the dominance of diesel-fueled farm tractors.

With no spark plug to compromise the combustion chamber, relying instead on tremendous compression ratios to heat and explode the air-fuel mixture, diesel engines offered a remarkable advantage over spark plug–ignited gas or kerosene engines in the production of horsepower and low-rpm torque. This advantage would ultimately make diesel synonymous with working equipment of any kind.

Still, through the early 1950s, the Deere line-up was mostly powered by other fuels, such as kerosene, gas, or even liquefied petroleum gas (LPG). Experimental diesel models had been in testing for nearly 10 years, but the company had

been reluctant to make such a radical change to successful products such as the Model A, Model D, and Model B. With its main competitors already offering strong diesel tractors in the market, however, Deere had no choice.

With the introduction of the Model R, John Deere made the leap to diesel. It was a big tractor, intended to replace the long-running Model D. The problem of cold-starting the Model R's powerful diesel engine was solved with a small gas pony engine, which took fire easily on cold mornings and used the heat from its exhaust to warm the diesel fuel and cylinders enough to make sparkless ignition possible.

With a whopping 50 percent improvement in pulling power over the Model D, the Model R was an immediate success in large farming operations.

The Model R was truly a tractor of distinction. Not only was it Deere's first diesel tractor, but it was the last tractor in Deere's alphabet naming system. Soon Deere's lettered tractors would be replaced with tractor designations based on multiples of 10.

Models 50 and 60 led the way. They were introduced in short succession in 1952 as replacements for Models A and B. The two new tractors were nestled in the same part of the Deere lineup, but with much greater power. They were not diesels, but they could be specified with "all fuel," LPG, or gasoline engines, sufficient for their needs in the low to midrange position in the Deere power lineup.

The replacement for the larger G came in the form of the Model 70. This tractor had plenty of power, especially when its diesel version was introduced in 1954.

These tractors were endowed with more than just grunt, however. Deere engineers figured out a way to produce a "live" or independent power take-off (PTO) and Powr-Trol tractor hydraulics. These features allowed an implement working behind the tractor not to be slowed by its operation, whether that was shifting the gears, stopping, or starting. These were valuable, practical features that made a difference in the everyday operation of the machine.

With the introduction of the Model 40 to replace the utility Model M, and the diesel Model 80 for the hefty Model R in 1955, Deere's transformation to a numbered roster of stout new tractors, each with useful new features, was complete. And its transformation into a purely diesel-powered tractor company was well underway.

Top and bottom: In the 1950s and 1960s, tractor manufacturers tried to outdo each other by making machines with more and more horsepower. When Deere introduced its first diesel, the Model R, in 1949, it proved a 50 percent improvement in pulling power over the Model D.

The first Deere Model R came off the production line at Waterloo in January 1949. There were just over 21,000 of them built before the production run ended in 1954 with a machine that pulled with 45.70 horses at the drawbar and sold for $3,650.

As Deere's first diesel, the Model R set a record for tractor fuel economy in its Nebraska tests. The big engine started with a two-cylinder, six-volt, nine-horsepower gasoline pony motor, which was mounted on top of the main engine's crankcase and cooled by its cooling system. Exhaust gases from the pony motor blew across the diesel's cylinders, heating them to aid diesel ignition.

A 1949 Model R with tiller. Typical of diesels, the compression ratio (16:1) on the Model R was much higher than its forebears, creating temperatures of about 1,000 degrees Fahrenheit in the combustion chamber. It had a five-speed transmission and a rated rpm of 1,000. *Voyageur Press Archives*

This 1952 version of the Model R displays its impressive bulk; the tractor weighed in at 7,400 pounds. It had a wheelbase of 85 inches, with 14x34-inch six-ply Champion Ground Grip tires on the back and 7.5x18-inch four-ply Guide Grip tires on the front.

Model R 1939–1955

Engine:	Two-cylinder overhead-valve diesel
Bore & Stroke:	5.75x8.00 inches
Engine speed:	1,000 rpm
Displacement:	416 ci
Power:	50.96 horsepower
Transmission:	Five-speed forward
Weight:	7,400 pounds

Above: A 1950 Model R with drill in action. With a Nebraska horsepower score of 45.70 and 51, drawbar and belt measure, and a maximum pull of 6,644 pounds, the Model R was an investment in high-production farming. It could plow a farmer's standard 40-acre paddock in 12 hours. *Voyageur Press Archives*

JOHN DEERE
Model "**R**"
DIESEL

THE COST-REDUCING TRACTOR
they're all talking about

Left: An advertisement displaying a local community of farmers examining the new Model R. It was the "cost reducing tractor they're all talking about." *Voyageur Press Archives*

JOHN DEERE

MOLINE, ILL.

A rough total of 33,000 John Deere Model 50 tractors, such as this one, were produced between 1952 and 1956. They came with a choice of three engines: a 27.5-drawbar horsepower gasoline engine, a 23.2-drawbar horsepower all-fuel engine, or a 29.2-drawbar horsepower LPG engine. The Model 50 sold for $2,011 in 1954.

Model 50 Standard 1952–1956

Engine:	Two-cylinder overhead-valve
Bore & Stroke:	4.69x5.50 inches
Engine speed:	1,250 rpm
Displacement:	190 ci
Power:	39 horsepower
Transmission:	Six-speed forward
Weight:	4,435 pounds

A detail shot of the Model 50, including its styled steering shaft housing and headlight. The Model 50 was an upgrade in many ways from the Model B it replaced. It had a robust Powr-Trol hydraulic system, which operated independently of both the PTO and the six-speed transmission.

The Model 50 insignia and radiator cover. A highly customized product, the Model 50 could be specified with four different front-end options, and it had adjustable rear tread. The tractor was 11 feet long, 5 feet tall, and weighed 4,435 pounds.

The Model 60 came in general purpose, standard-tread, orchard, and high-crop versions. The evening light just illuminates its rack-and-pinion rear wheel tread, another Model 60 innovation.

Model 60 Standard 1952–1956	
Engine:	Two-cylinder overhead-valve
Bore & Stroke:	5.50x6.75 inches
Engine speed:	975 rpm
Displacement:	321 ci
Power:	38.02 horsepower
Transmission:	Six-speed forward
Weight:	5,300 pounds

Sleek fenders protect this Model 60 Orchard from entanglement in branches. Produced alongside the Model 50, the Model 60 sold about 60,000 units from 1952 to 1957, at a final asking price of $2,500.

Along with the Model 50, the Model 60 was the debut of Deere's new duplex carburetion, which provided a separate carburetor for each cylinder, enabling improvement in horsepower and efficiency. This Model 60 Orchard came with a choice of three engines: a 36.9-drawbar horsepower gasoline powerplant, a 30.1-drawbar horsepower all-fuel engine, or a 38.1 drawbar horsepower LPG engine. All had a rated rpm of 975. *Hans Halberstadt*

Originally conceived as a replacement for the Model G, the Model 70 was endowed with a completely new engine and a variety of upgrades and new features. Produced from 1953 to 1956, the Model 70 cost $3,000 in 1956. More than 40,000 were built during its production life.

The Model 70 was initially issued as a gas, all-fuel, or LPG engine tractor; then, in November 1954, the Model 70 Diesel (shown here) was unveiled. It was Deere's first diesel for the row-crop farmer. The new engine displaced 376 cubic inches and could produce 45.7 horsepower at the drawbar. A redesigned, 18-cubic-inch starter motor was used to get it going, which revved at a very fast 5,500 rpm to quickly heat up the main powerplant. *Voyageur Press Archives*

A Model 70 with Model 50 Loader demonstrates the ever-widening application of tractor power. With the loader mounted, the Model 70 weighed well over 6,000 pounds and measured 11 feet, 4 inches long, standing on 38-inch rear tires and 16-inch front tires. *Voyageur Press Archives*

Model 70 1953–1956	
Engine:	Two-cylinder overhead-valve
Bore & Stroke:	6.125x7.00 inches
Engine speed:	975 rpm
Displacement:	412.5 ci
Power:	45/51.5 horsepower
Transmission:	Six-speed forward
Weight:	6,035 pounds

Above: The dependable John Deere Model 70 High-Crop was a strong commercial success in the mid-1950s. It incorporated most of the features of Models 50 and 60, including their advanced hydraulics.

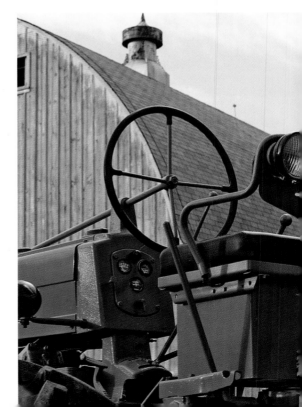

Right: This Model 70 High-Crop could reach 2.5 miles per hour in first gear, 8.75 miles per hour in fifth, and 12.5 miles per hour in sixth gear. The transmission was engaged by a dry multiple-disc clutch, which was operated by a hand lever, just visible in this picture. Rear-tread width could be adjusted from a minimum of 60 inches to a maximum of 88 inches. *Randy Leffingwell*

The power steering system used a hydraulic pump powered by the engine to ease the effort required to turn the heavy wheels in soft soil such as this. *Randy Leffingwell*

Model M Series 1947–1955	
Engine:	Two-cylinder vertical
Bore & Stroke:	4.00x4.00 inches
Engine Speed:	1,650 rpm
Displacement:	100.5 ci
Power:	20.45 horsepower
Transmission:	Four-speed forward
Weight:	2,560 pounds

Like all Model 70s, the high-crop version shown here was manufactured at the Waterloo tractor facility, where, for the first time, power steering could be installed at the buyer's option (so indicated under the model number). *Voyageur Press Archives*

This 1955 Model 80 has been fitted with an aftermarket cab—a testament to the emerging concern for operator comfort seen in the 1950s. This tractor came only in its standard version. Although power steering was technically an option, very few tractors were built without it. *Randy Leffingwell*

Model 80 1955–1956

Engine:	Two-cylinder overhead-valve
Bore & Stroke:	6.125x8.00 inches
Engine speed:	1,125 rpm
Displacement:	472 ci
Power:	67.6 PTO horsepower
Transmission:	Six-speed forward
Weight:	8,150 pounds

The Model 80 was introduced as a replacement for the Model R, Deere's first diesel, incorporating the new features that had improved the performance of Models 50, 60, and 70, and providing a welcome increase of 17 horsepower.

LANZ Diesel D 6016

In 1956, John Deere acquired the German tractor manufacturer, Lanz, maker of this Lanz Diesel 6016. By acquiring Lanz, Deere gained a European manufacturing site, as it was the only U.S. tractor producer without a European factory. *Voyageur Press Archives*

Opposite page:
Top: Lanz is best known for its Bulldog tractor. It was unveiled in 1921 by Karl Lanz, son of company founder Heinrich Lanz and designed by Fritz Huber. *Voyageur Press Archives*

Bottom: A brochure for the 1906 and 2706 Lanz Bulldog models. The original Lanz Bulldog was revolutionary because it was the world's first hot bulb–fired tractor burning inexpensive crude oil. *Voyageur Press Archives*

LANZ

E 2530 e.

Sectional view of Low Pressure Tyred "All Purpose Tractor"
with six speeds forward and electric equipment

The End of
the Two-Cylinder Era

In 1956, Deere replaced its Model 70 with the Model 720. Advancements included Custom Powr-Trol hydraulics, which enabled more precise positioning of implements, and Load and Depth Control, which kept implements at a uniform soil depth. The distinctive coloring of the 20 Series, well displayed on the engine and radiator cover of this 720 diesel, sets it apart from other models.

Chapter 6

As the 1950s waned and a new decade approached, Deere & Company stood on the brink of a major transformation.

The company had been quietly cultivating a radically new product line of multi-cylinder powered tractors, which it intended to unveil as a single group, instead of piecemeal. The launch had originally been planned for 1958, but development work was running behind schedule and delayed the presentation until late 1960.

In the meantime, Deere engineers and industrial designers produced some excellent work in terms of new features and tractor style concepts; these were incorporated into Deere's 20 and 30 Series: the last of the two-cylinder Deeres.

Even a cursory examination of the 20 Series—which includes the 320, 420, 420 Crawler, 520, 620, 720, and 820 models—reveals an attractive new look and capability. That Deere & Company could produce such a successful line, even as it was building toward a dramatic conversion to its New Generation of tractors, says something about the level of corporate strength it had achieved by the late 1950s.

The 20 Series provided horsepower improvements all across the board, while also setting records at University of Nebraska tractor performance tests for fuel consumption through better design and more precise manufacturing.

And with the introduction of an innovative hydraulic system, Custom Powr-Trol on the 20 Series, Deere had a feature that really made a difference in the field. Farmers at the time were struggling with inconsistent depth and pitch of tractor-pulled implements and the sheer effort required to set and adjust the implements.

Custom Powr-Trol offered farmers simple and convenient hydraulic control over the height and attitude of implements, and it could "remember" previous settings. That meant that at the end of a row, an implement could be lifted for the turn and then replaced exactly as it had been before, making the fieldwork consistent.

And Deere got serious about operator comfort. It brought in Dr. Janet Travell of the Harvard University Medical Center (better known as President John F. Kennedy's back specialist) to help isolate the driver from the wild bumps and jolts inherent in tractor work. The resulting Float-Ride seat adjusted damping to each individual's body mass, and it provided a level of comfort unmatched in the industry.

Beyond its technical improvements, the 20 Series is considered by some to be Deere's most visually appealing line. The tractors were given a stately appearance with integrated lines and solid yellow bars along the engine cover and radiator side panels, giving contrast to the dark green John Deere logo and model number.

With the 20 Series selling well on the strength of its added power and features, and the long-awaited New Generation tracking for a rollout in late 1960, a final line of two-cylinder tractors was introduced in 1958: the 30 Series. This group of tractors included the 330, 430, 530, 630, 730, and 830 models.

Building on the human factors taken into consideration while engineering the previous series, the 30 group was more comfortable and practical to use. A step and handgrips were added to aid mounting and dismounting. Also added were an improved seat and broader platform and a more modern dashboard, which straddled the steering column. All these features made these tractors better working partners.

In a development to presage the operator amenities of modern tractors, some Deere tractors began to offer an optional Weather Brake cab, which did not offer full enclosure, but sheltered the operator from the elements. These were popular marketable advancements, as the buyer and operator of the tractor were usually one and the same.

Unknown to agricultural America, as these two-cylinder tractors chugged into fields across the country, Deere was adding the finishing touches to a new set of revolutionary tractors and already planning their introduction. This New Generation would set a benchmark for the industry, but it would also mark the end of a charming and historic era of two-cylinder power at the world's premier tractor company.

While Deere & Company engineers were secretly developing the revolutionary New Generation line, they were still producing two-cylinder classics, including the 30 Series tractors that were introduced in 1958.

The Model 420 replaced the Model 40 with a more powerful, fuel-efficient tractor based on a redesigned cylinder head and pistons. It had a Nebraska drawbar horsepower rating (rated load measure) of 20 and a 100-percent drawbar power measure of 27 horsepower. Its rated belt horsepower was 24, with a maximum power belt horsepower of 29.

Model 420 Standard All-Fuel 1956–1958	
Engine:	Two-cylinder overhead-valve
Bore & Stroke:	4.25x4 inches
Engine speed:	1,850 rpm
Displacement:	113.5 ci
Power:	23.5 PTO horsepower
Transmission:	Four-speed forward
Weight:	2,750 pounds

This Model 420 is easy to identify as a propane gas–powered version. This tractor's engine was the same size as the gas fuel engines, with a bore and stroke of 4.25x4.00 inches and a displacement of 113 cubic inches. It turned over at 1,850 rpm.

Front detail, Model 420, propane version. Conspicuous in this photograph is the lettering on the top of the radiator housing announcing the tractor's power steering, which now came standard on the machine. More than 55,000 420s were built at Deere's Dubuque factory between 1956 and 1958.

Variations of the Model 620 included the 620 general purpose, 620S, 620H, and the tractor pictured, the Model 620 Orchard. Front-end options were dual narrow, dual Roll-O-Matic, wide front, or single wheel. In 1956, a new Model 620 cost $3,003.

This unusual-looking machine is a propane-driven Model 620 Orchard, with fenders better designed than previous models' to prevent entanglement of fruit tree branches. Propane was a successful tractor fuel in the 1950s, partly due to its price and better compression ratio.

Model 620 RC All-Fuel 1956–1958	
Engine:	Two-cylinder overhead-valve
Bore & Stroke:	5.50x6.375 inches
Engine speed:	1,125 rpm
Displacement:	302.9 ci
Power:	35.68 belt horsepower
Transmission:	Six-speed forward
Weight:	5,858 pounds

A Model 620 with disc hooked up to the tractor's new universal three-point hitch. On sloping land such as this, the 620's hydraulic system with Load and Depth Control could help keep each pass down the rows consistent. *Voyageur Press Archives*

The Model 720 diesel was a powerhouse; it was advertised as a five-plow tractor capable of replacing two smaller tractors. Its engine was essentially the same as the one on the Model 70 diesel it replaced, but its transmission was upgraded to a new six-speed with a creeper gear.

Model 720 RC Diesel 1952–1956	
Engine:	Two-cylinder overhead-valve
Bore & Stroke:	6.125x6.375 inches
Engine speed:	1,125 rpm
Displacement:	376 ci
Power:	56.84 belt horsepower
Transmission:	Six-speed forward
Weight:	7,800 pounds

The new Deere logo on the Model 720. Deere & Company underwent seven logo redesigns in the twentieth century, all featuring a leaping deer and the company name.

The rear wheel hub of a Model 720 diesel.

A propane-powered version of the Model 720. It had a crosswise-mounted crankshaft, ran at 1,125 rpm, and produced a compression ratio of 8:1. At its Nebraska test, this tractor produced 51 belt horsepower for one hour at its rated load and put out 57 horsepower for two hours at 100-percent maximum load.

A Model 720 tractor with its propane tank clearly visible below the sky. The Model 720 had an oil-washed, wire mesh air cleaner and a replaceable, paper-element oil filter, and a variable-speed centrifugal governor.

This photograph shows the light script font used on the 20 Series model numbers, which enhanced the bold, block lettering of the company name across the side of the engine cover.

The Model 430T (T for tricycle configuration) could be specified with gasoline, all-fuel, or LP engines. In fact, the 430 was so customized that some dealers referred to it as a "fleet." The 430 could be ordered as the 430S (standard), 430U (utility), 430W (row crop utility), 430H (high crop), 430V (special), 430 F3 (forklift), and 430C (crawler).

Model 430 Standard All-Fuel 1959–1960

Engine:	Two-cylinder overhead-valve
Bore & Stroke:	4.25x4 inches
Engine speed:	1,850 rpm
Displacement:	113.5 ci
Power:	23.5 PTO horsepower
Transmission:	Four-speed forward
Weight:	2,750 pounds

The Model 430T posed before a row of corn. A total of 3,264 Model 430T tractors were built at Deere's Dubuque, Iowa, plant between 1958 and 1960, out of a nearly 15,000 Model 430s overall. Standard equipment was a four-speed transmission, but it could be ordered with a five-speed. In 1959, a new Model 430 cost $2,500.

The Model 430, wide-front version. A particularly useful feature on the Model 430 was its optional direction reverser, operated by a clutch. It enabled the operator to go backward or forward in the same gear without shifting the transmission. This feature endeared it to many farmers, as it made a number of farm chores easier.

This Model 530 appears different than the tractor it replaced, the 520, although inside the two tractors were similar. It has dual headlights as opposed to the 520's singles, a much different font used for the model number, and more yellow sheet metal along the engine.

Model 530 All-Fuel 1959–1960

Engine:	Two-cylinder overhead-valve
Bore & Stroke:	4.69x5.50 inches
Engine speed:	1,325 rpm
Displacement:	190 ci
Power:	26.6 belt horsepower
Transmission:	Six-speed forward
Weight:	4,960 pounds

The Model 530's stylish dual headlights and sleek fenders.

The Model 530's Roll-O-Matic front end and its 5.5-inch-wide, 16-inch-diameter front wheels. Other front end options were single and wide front.

The John Deere Model 630 was similar enough to the Model 620 to be given the same Nebraska test, with rated-load horsepower ratings of 44 at the drawbar and 48 at the belt. It was available as a row-crop, standard, and high-crop tractor. Visible in this picture is its characteristic yellow seat back cushion with logo.

Model 630RC All-Fuel 1959–1960

Engine:	Two-cylinder overhead-valve
Bore & Stroke:	5.50x6.375 inches
Engine speed:	1,125 rpm
Displacement:	302.9 ci
Power:	35.68 horsepower
Transmission:	Six-speed forward
Weight:	5,858 pounds

The Model 630 was presented by dealers as a full four-plow tractor on the strength of its powerful engine, customized to the fuel preference of the customer. Overwhelmingly, most farmers specified gas (15,940 tractors sold), followed by propane (1,918 tractors sold), and then all-fuel (202 tractors sold).

A Model 630 at work in the field. This tractor would have cost its owner $3,300 in 1958. Of the three available versions of the Model 630, most farmers bought the general purpose version (17,224); far fewer bought the standard 630 (735), and only 16 bought the high-crop 630. *Voyageur Press Archives*

The Model 730 was a flexible fuel machine; it could be ordered as a gas, LPG (shown here), diesel, or all-fuel tractor. The gasoline engine could muster 53 drawbar horsepower, the all-fuel version 41 drawbar horsepower, and the LPG and the diesel could make 54 drawbar horsepower. In 1960, the final year of production, the Model 730 sold for $3,700.

The John Deere Model 730 could be ordered as a row-crop, standard, or high-crop tractor, such as the one pictured here. Independent PTO, power steering, and a comfy Float Ride seat all came standard on this model.

Model 730 RC Diesel 1959–1960

Engine:	Two-cylinder overhead-valve
Bore & Stroke:	6.125x6.375 inches
Engine speed:	1,125 rpm
Displacement:	376 ci
Power:	56.84 horsepower
Transmission:	Six-speed forward
Weight:	7,800 pounds

The Model 730 diesel at work with a plow. This version of the John Deere Model 730 sold more than 22,000 units between 1958 and 1961. The tractor pictured here had an optional 18-cubic-inch V-4 gas pony engine to help with cold starting its two-cylinder, 376-cubic-inch diesel. *Voyageur Press Archives*

The beautiful 1959 John Deere Model 830 developed just under 70 horsepower at the drawbar. It could be started with either a four-cylinder gasoline pony engine or a 24-volt electric starter. The Model 830 production run lasted until 1960 and more than 6,700 machines were produced.

Model 830 Diesel 1959–1960	
Engine:	Two-cylinder diesel
Bore & Stroke:	6.125x8 inches
Engine speed:	1,125 rpm
Displacement:	472 ci
Power:	75.6 horsepower
Transmission:	Six-speed forward
Weight:	8,150 pounds

The Model 830 diesel with its two-cylinder, 6.125x8-inch bore-and-stroke engine was never given a Nebraska tractor test, as its performance was practically identical to the previously tested Model 820.

The Deere logo and power steering emblem of a Model 830 diesel. Power steering, made possible by recent advances in hydraulics, was a desirable feature on a large tractor such as the 830.

The lettering on a Model 830 diesel. In the late 1950s, the shadow-style font chosen for the 30 Series tractors was considered bold and altogether modern.

The New Generation

The Model 1010 was part of the grand
unveiling of Deere's New Generation of Power
in Dallas on August 30, 1960. It was built at
Deere's Dubuque, Iowa, factory until 1965,
when the tractor could be bought for $3,500.
Chester Peterson Jr.

Chapter 7

By the middle of 1960, word had spread in the farm community that Deere & Company was on the verge of a big announcement. It was hard to believe the rumors. After 40 years of two-cylinder power, could Deere really be introducing tractors with four and six cylinders?

That question was answered emphatically at a spectacular gala on August 30, 1960.

The company spent approximately $1.25 million and two years' planning on the coming-out party alone; the choreography of the introduction had been rehearsed in a full-scale mock-up arena in Moline. Over 5,000 dealers, industry leaders, and company personnel were brought together from across the country in lavish style for the one-day event at the Dallas Memorial Auditorium.

There they witnessed the dawn of a new age at Deere. One gleaming John Deere tractor after another chugged across the auditorium floor, all of them with newly designed engines.

It was the end of Johnny Popper and the beginning of a new tradition. After building over a million two-cylinder tractors, Deere was retiring the basic concept of the powerplants that had brought the company to its penultimate position in the industry, behind International Harvester. Still, it was hoped that this bright new line of hard-charging machines would finally make Deere number one in sales. Within a few short years, that hope was realized.

The first of the New Generation tractors was the 10 Series, the smallest of which was the gas- or diesel-powered 35-horsepower Model 1010, followed by the 2010, the 3010, the 4010, the 5010, and the largest, the enormous four-wheel-drive, 8010. These tractors were all four- and six-cylinder models with attractive new features based on rapid advancements in hydraulics.

Hydraulic pumps, motors, and circuitry elements had been vastly improved in the 1950s, and the New Generation tractors reaped obvious benefits in terms of precise control of implements and new features such as power brakes and power steering. The tractor Model 4010, for instance, offered simultaneous operation of three different live hydraulic circuits.

In keeping with the successful ideas of the past, the tractors were highly customized, available in diesel, gas, or LPG versions, and with different row-crop frame configurations and adjustable front ends.

Almost immediately after the introduction of the 10 Series, models from the 20 Series began to replace these initial New Generation tractors. The 8020 came in 1961, and the 3020 and 4020 in 1963. Not only did these new models have increased power, but they came with a Power-Shift transmission option, which could change gears easily without the use of a clutch and had a hydraulic-powered differential lock. The 20 Series could also be ordered with hydraulic-powered front-wheel drive.

In 1971, Deere introduced the last of this series, the Model 7020. It wasn't Deere's first four-wheel-drive tractor, but due to the limited success of the Model 8010 (only 100 of that four-wheel-drive model were built), the 7020 is often mistaken for Deere's first. Powering its four wheels was a big six-cylinder diesel rated at 145 horsepower at the PTO.

Playing on the resounding success of the New Generation line, the next family of tractors (starting with models 4030, 4230, 4430, and 4630) was launched as Generation II, on August 19, 1972, in New Orleans. These tractors offered the healthy increase in horsepower the market was demanding, with even more power to follow in the subsequently released 175-horsepower 8430 and 225-horsepower 8630, both with articulated four-wheel-drives.

The salient feature on these tractors was their enclosed driving compartments, or Sound-Gard bodies, which protected the operator against sound, rain, cold, heat, and, most importantly, death or injury in a rollover accident.

Deere had introduced optional Roll-Gard ROPS six years earlier in 1966, and it had been one of the company's least popular innovations. No other tractors had it, and farmers felt they didn't need it. Although Deere had heavily researched and developed the feature, it decided to give the technology to its competitors, which led to its universal acceptance in the marketplace by the early 1970s. Without question, hundreds of farmers are alive today due to that decision.

Impressive Generation II achievements continued in the mid-1970s as Deere upgraded the entire line with the 40 Series. The larger tractors in this group were named the Iron Workhorses. These ranged from the smallest, the 90-horsepower 4040 up to the 180-horsepower 4840. These powerful new machines offered, as Deere's marketing department proclaimed, "more horses from more iron."

Deere & Company certainly created a spectacle when introducing its first four- and six-cylinder New Generation tractors. The tractors motored across an arena filled with more than 5,000 Deere dealers, industry leaders, and guests on August 30, 1960, in Dallas, Texas.

Hydraulic technology was advancing by leaps and bounds in the 1950s and 1960s. The Model 1010 had an open-center pump to power its multifunctional hydraulics and optional power steering (although due to its smaller size, few models were ordered with it). It could be ordered with a remote hydraulic cylinder for control of either rear- or front-mounted equipment. *Chester Peterson Jr.*

Model 1010 1960–1965

Engine:	Four-cylinder gas
Bore & Stroke:	3.50x3.00 inches
Engine speed:	2,500 rpm
Displacement:	115.5 ci
Power:	36.13 PTO horsepower
Transmission:	Five-speed forward
Weight:	4,000 pounds

This Model 1010 has 34-inch rear tires, 15-inch front tires, and a 70-inch wheelbase, and it weighs about 4,000 pounds. The 1010 had an optional, dual-speed (540 and 1,000 rpm) PTO, a five-speed transmission, and came in a variety of configurations—row-crop (R), orchard (O), utility (U), and industrial wheel (W), as well as a crawler, which sold over 15,000 units. *Chester Peterson Jr.*

Two industrial versions of the 1010 were produced: the 1010 industrial crawler and this 1010 wheel tractor. The 1010 wheel was styled more like a farm tractor than other industrial versions, but it had a heavy-duty front axle, which, like the rear tread, was not adjustable. Its hydraulics and PTO could be removed if necessary. *Chester Peterson Jr.*

With either a gas or diesel engine specified, the 1010 produced 29.16 horsepower at the drawbar (35.99 horsepower at the belt), enough to pull this Model 475 plow through hard-baked soil. *Voyageur Press Archives*

The classic New Generation tractor, a Model 2010, was built at Deere's Dubuque, Iowa, factory. It could be specified with a gasoline or LPG engine—bored and stroked in four cylinders to a 144.5-cubic-inch displacement—or a 165.1-cubic-inch diesel. *Chester Peterson Jr.*

Model 2010 1960–1965	
Engine:	Four-cylinder gas
Bore & Stroke:	3.625x3.50 inches
Engine speed:	2,500 rpm
Displacement:	144.5 ci
Power:	46.86 PTO horsepower
Transmission:	Eight-speed forward
Weight:	4,800 pounds

The row-crop version was the most successful variant of the 2010 tractor, with over 17,000 units sold, mostly with gasoline-burning engines, followed closely by the row-crop utility version with just over 16,000. It weighed 4,800 pounds and had an 87-inch wheelbase. Deere also offered a 2010 Special at a lower price. It was only available with a diesel engine. *Chester Peterson Jr.*

This specialist high-crop Model 2010 found a small niche in the market, selling about 500 units. It had a top speed of about 20 miles per hour in its "road gear," and it came with Deere's Synchro-Range transmission, with eight gears forward and three reverse. The tractor was available with either a gas, diesel (16-gallon tank), or LPG engine. The four-cylinder powerplant had a PTO horsepower rating of 46.86 and a rated rpm of 2,500. *Chester Peterson Jr.*

This John Deere Model 3010 pulled with 52.0 drawbar horsepower (rated load) and 55.09 PTO horsepower at its Nebraska test, with its 201-cubic-inch gasoline engine with a 7.5:1 compression ratio. Its 254-cubic-inch diesel had a compression ratio of 16:1. Note the fenders, inset head-lights, and the cushiony "deluxe" seat, all part of the carefully crafted styling of early 1960s Deere tractors. *Chester Peterson Jr.*

Model 3010 1961–1963	
Engine:	Four-cylinder gas
Bore & Stroke:	4.0x4.0 inches
Engine speed:	2,200 rpm
Displacement:	201 ci
Power:	55.09 PTO horsepower
Transmission:	Eight-speed forward
Weight:	5,800 pounds

A total of 44,000 Model 3010 tractors were built at Deere's Waterloo, Iowa, plant. The 3010 had a closed-center hydraulic pump moving 18 gallons per minute through two outlets, with a capacity fill of 9.5 gallons. This revolutionary new four-plow tractor sold for $4,700 in 1963. *Chester Peterson Jr.*

These two tractors, Models 3010 and 4010, were what many refer to as the first of the "real" New Generation tractors. Although the 1010 and the 2010 were introduced alongside them, it was the 3010 and the 4010 that incorporated the innovative characteristics of the new tractor line, such as multiple, independent hydraulic circuits and a Syncro-Range transmission. *Chester Peterson Jr.*

JOHN DEERE
MOLINE, ILL.

This 80.96-horsepower Model 4010 had a six-cylinder engine, displacing between 302 and 380 cubic inches, depending on fuel type: gas, diesel, or LPG. It was a truly modern tractor, with an instrument panel that included a speed-hour meter, an electric fuel gauge, oil pressure and generator current indicators, and a light switch. *Chester Peterson Jr.*

On the 4010, the fuel tank was moved to the very front of the tractor, a design tweak Deere said would reduce fuel evaporation and make cold starting easier. The 4010's distinctive red fuel cap can just be seen on the left side of the front end of the hood. *Chester Peterson Jr.*

Model 4010 1960–1963

Engine:	Six-cylinder gas
Bore & Stroke:	4.0x4.0 inches
Engine speed:	2,200 rpm
Displacement:	302 ci
Power:	80.96 PTO horsepower
Transmission:	Eight-speed forward
Weight:	6,980 pounds

The entire 10 Series lineup was brought together for this shot taken in 1950. A few easily identified machines are the 1010 crawler in the foreground, a 4010 LPG with its bulbous nose in the second row, and the mammoth 8010 at the far right. *Voyageur Press Archives*

The Model 8010 was a truly innovative tractor, as Deere's first tractor with mechanical four-wheel-drive, but only about 100 Model 8010 tractors were made before the production run was halted in 1960. Transmission problems forced the company to convert these into 8020s with heavier duty transmissions and clutches.

Model 8010 1960	
Engine:	Six-cylinder gas
Bore & Stroke:	4.50x5.0 inches
Engine speed:	2,100 rpm
Displacement:	425 ci
Power:	150 drawbar horsepower
Transmission:	Nine-speed forward
Weight:	19,700 pounds

One of the first articulated farm tractors for Deere, this Model 8010 took some getting used to on the part of the operator. The tractor weighed almost 10 tons with a wheelbase of 10 feet and a height of over 8 feet, but power was not a problem. *Voyageur Press Archives*

A brochure advertising the mighty Model 8010. *Voyageur Press Archives*

The Model 2020 was truly an international tractor, being built in factories in Mexico; Baden-Wurttemberg, Germany; and Dubuque. It was issued in 1965 as a replacement for the 2010, with a new collar shift transmission featuring eight forward speeds and four in reverse.
Randy Leffingwell

The 2020 came in gasoline or diesel versions, both four-cylinder engines of similar horsepower and rpm rating. They both used pressure lubrication and water cooling, with thermostat control and fixed bypass. The 2020's new Type II three-point hitch is shown clearly here.

The Model 2020 was offered with an optional dual-speed PTO, which was handy when linked up with implements such as this Model 37 mower. *Voyageur Press Archives*

Above: The Model 4020 is considered one of the classic Deere creations partly due to its practical utility, as evidenced in this photo. With nearly 100 horsepower available at the PTO and smooth-operating multifunctional hydraulics, this tractor could do it all. *Chester Peterson Jr.*

Left: The shifter for the 4020's Syncro-Range transmission, which was engaged by a foot-operated, spring-loaded 12-inch dry-disc clutch. Optional was an eight-forward, four-reverse Power-Shift transmission, with a multiple wet-disc clutch. *Chester Peterson Jr.*

Left: Instrumentation had come a long way by the time the New Generation tractors were designed. This Model 4020 had a speed-hour meter, fuel gauge, engine temperature gauge, engine oil pressure light, alternator light, transmission temperature gauge, and transmission oil pressure light (Power Shift model). It even had a cigar lighter. *Chester Peterson Jr.*

Below: A Model 4020 making use of its closed-center variable displacement hydraulic pump, which either assisted or actuated its steering, brakes, differential lock, and optional Power Shift transmission.

The high-crop version of the 4020. Shipping weight on the 4020 High-Crop with all equipment in the box was 8,985 pounds for the gas-powered version, 9,170 for the LPG version, and 9,235 for the diesel version. *Chester Peterson Jr.*

Model 4020 1963–1972	
Engine:	Six-cylinder gas
Bore & Stroke:	4.25x4.25 inches
Engine speed:	2,200 rpm
Displacement:	362 ci
Power:	88.1 PTO horsepower
Transmission:	Eight-speed forward
Weight:	8,865 pounds

The movement toward operator comfort and safety took a large step forward with the common appearance of cabs on tractors, such as this 4020. The cab included rollover protection, which saved many a farmer's life.

Oddly enough, this cozy cab, optional equipment on this Model 4020, was a hard sell for years before it began catching on in the late 1960s and early 1970s.

Above: Plain to see, the Model 7020 was a heavy-duty, articulated four-wheel-drive tractor with lots of muscle. It weighed over seven tons and produced 146.17 maximum horsepower at the PTO with its six-cylinder turbocharged and intercooled diesel engine, displacing 404 cubic inches. *Chester Peterson Jr.*

Right: A view inside the Sound-Gard cab of the 7020 with its upgraded ergonomic seat. *Randy Leffingwell*

The Model 8020 was a rebuilt 8010 with a beefier drivetrain, which included an oil-cooled heavy-duty four-plate clutch, which was hydraulically activated. It was a large machine in its own right, with 106 gallons in the fuel tank, 15 gallons in the transmission housing, 12 gallons flowing through the radiator, and 4.5 gallons in the crankcase. *Chester Peterson Jr.*

The hydraulic system on the 8020 used a large 60-gallon-per-minute pump, with a reservoir of 25 gallons. Its electrical system began with a 24-volt starter, using 12 volts for its four front lights (two head and two flood) and four rear lights (two red tail and two flood). A nice upgrade for the operator was Deere's posture design seat, evident in this photo. *Chester Peterson Jr.*

Built between 1994 and 1998,
the Waterloo-built John Deere Model 8100
is a high-production machine delivering
160 horsepower to the PTO with a
six-cylinder turbo diesel.

Modern Machining Marvels

Chapter 8

After the oil shocks of the 1970s, farmers were reeling in the early 1980s because of depressed commodity prices and high fuel bills. With fuel economy an imperative on the farm, Deere launched its 50 Series tractors with upgraded engines. These new efficient tractors, sourced both from the Waterloo plant and Deere's factory in Mannheim, Germany, ranged in power from the 45-horsepower 2150 all the way up to the massive, 274-drawbar-horsepower 8850 turbo-diesel, which displaced almost a thousand cubic inches.

Deere had invested heavily in its new power-plants, whose horsepower ratings soared to new heights on the strength of new technologies, such as intercooled charge air, which produced a denser air-fuel mixture for hotter, more powerful, and more efficient combustion.

Another new technology attracting customers to Deere tractors was mechanical four-wheel-drive, offered on all 50 Series models from the 2350 up to the six-cylinder, 162-drawbar-horsepower 4850. Such innovations helped the tractor company keep customers' attention and enthusiasm through a difficult time in American agricultural history.

With the arrival of the 55 Series in 1987, the worst of the farm depression was over, and Deere celebrated its new tractor line in style. It had been 150 years since John Deere had begun making plows in Grand Detour, Illinois, and the company had grown to become the largest and the best farm equipment manufacturer in the world. The new tractors and a rebounding economy helped Deere post its first profit in three years in 1988, setting a record at $315 million.

As it had on the 50 Series, Deere's tractor plant in Mannheim handled a large share of the new lineup, as well as Deere's facility in Saltillo, Mexico, and its traditional facilities at Dubuque and Waterloo.

Introduction of the biggest machines in the series was delayed until 1989, when the 4055, 4255, and the company's mammoth row-crop tractor, the 200-PTO-horsepower, inline-six turbo-diesel 4955, were introduced. Even larger were the tractors of Deere's 60 Series that followed, ranging in size all the way up to the 322-horsepower Model 8960.

The tractor market had been changing since the 1960s in the United States, and Deere's gigantic new tractors reflected it. Small farms were consolidating into even larger agricultural businesses, which required high-production equipment to handle the new scale of operations. In 1992, the company announced an "All New Breed of Power," which would be incorporated into its 5000, 6000, and 7000 Series tractors. These tractors had modern features that provided unheard-of productivity. The market response was immediate, as Deere market share soared in North America and Europe. In Germany, for the first time, Deere moved into first place in tractor sales.

Electronic engine control was the key to Deere's improvements in power and efficiency, as well as tremendous new capabilities in engine diagnostics

After the farm crisis of the early 1980s, Deere & Company focused on building larger and larger tractors for increasingly consolidated farming efforts. As part of that initiative, the company introduced "an all new breed of power" tractor line in 1992. *Voyageur Press Archives*

and maintenance. With an electronic brain keeping track of vital engine data, optimizing fuel flow, adjusting valve timing, and fine-tuning performance, tractors such as the 350-PTO-horsepower Model 8870, part of the mega-sized 70 Series, became a reality.

At the same time, the compact end of the tractor market was growing, fed in part by Deere's new plant in Augusta, Georgia, constructed in 1992 and dedicated to 40-, 50-, and 60-horsepower machines.

Innovation was everywhere as the new millennium approached. In late 1996, in an attempt to reduce ground compaction (which is always a problem in the field after a tractor pass), Deere tried something no other tractor manufacturer had thought of: rubber tracks. With flexible tracks added, the 8100 and the 8400 became the 8100T and the 8400T. Later, in 1999, rubber-tracked models were incorporated with Deere's new 9000 Series as well.

John Deere moved into the twenty-first century with the new Twenty Series tractors. These machines were built with the same dedication to quality and innovation that marked the Deere company from its inception, when the legendary agricultural manufacturer was in the hands of one man: John Deere.

The John Deere 1630, produced between 1973 and 1979, had a three-cylinder, 179-cubic-inch engine with a rated horsepower of 50 at the PTO. Power was communicated through an eight-forward-speed, four-reverse-speed transmission. *Voyageur Press Archives*

Model 4430 1973–1977

Engine:	Six-cylinder diesel-turbo
Engine speed:	2,200 rpm
Displacement:	404 ci
Power:	125.88 PTO horsepower
Transmission:	Eight-speed forward
Weight:	9,930 pounds

Not exactly a cab, but a strong shelter with ROPS keeps the operator shaded on this Model 2130, powered by a four-cylinder, 239-cubic-inch, 66-PTO-horsepower diesel. This tractor has an optional 16-speed transmission and weighs just under three tons. *Voyageur Press Archives*

4430-Turbo-Charged Power handles more work

John Deere's 4430 is a tractor that's built for turbo-charged power. The engine, 149 h.p., transmission, final drives—even the lubrication and cooling systems—were designed with turbo-charging in mind. And that makes a big difference in reliability.

The turbo-charger, for example, is mounted in the centre of the engine, so that every cylinders gets an equal charge of air—giving you more power and better fuel economy.

You may choose to equip the 4430 with power front-wheel-drive—you won't lose valuable ground clearance because it's hydrostatic. Individual hydraulic motors are tucked inside each front wheel, protected and ready to deliver power the instant you need it—with shifting on-the-go.

The 4430 also has Perma-Clutch that's cooled by constant oil circulation. It's a wet disc clutch that never needs adjustment; virtually a lifetime clutch.

There's a choice of four power-matched transmissions and many options such as Power Weight Transfer Hitch—and remote cylinder outlets.

Rice, wheat, maize or whatever crop and work you have, the 4430 is equal to the challenge.

A brochure heralding the dawn of the turbo diesel tractor. In the 30 Series, the 4030 and 4230 were normally aspirated gas or diesel engines, but this 4430 had Deere's new turbocharger on its six-cylinder diesel engine, and thus enjoyed an increase in horsepower. *Voyageur Press Archives*

A John Deere 2640 emerges from an orchard. This tractor was manufactured between 1976 and 1983, when it was priced at $22,000. It delivered 70 horsepower to its PTO, which could be set at 540 rpm or 1,000 rpm. *Voyageur Press Archives*

Model 2040 Standard 1981–1987	
Engine:	Four-cylinder diesel
Bore & Stroke:	4.193x4.331 inches
Engine speed:	2,500 rpm
Displacement:	239.2 ci
Power:	75 horsepower
Transmission:	Sixteen-speed forward
Weight:	7,848 pounds

2040S Tractor

Built between 1981 and 1987, the 2040S offered a reasonably priced four-cylinder diesel with 75 horsepower. It weighed 7,584 pounds (8,245 for the optional four-wheel-drive version) and stood 7.5 feet tall. *Voyageur Press Archives*

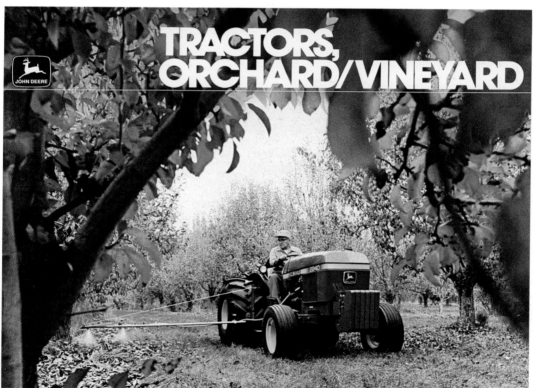

TRACTORS, ORCHARD/VINEYARD

A brochure outlining all the standard features and options for the 2040 to 2640 orchard tractors. *Voyageur Press Archives*

Part of the 50 Series, which came out in the 1980s, the Model 4450 met the increased horsepower demands of the market with a 466-cubic-inch, six-cylinder turbo-diesel engine rated at 140 horsepower at the PTO. *Voyageur Press Archives*

In 1988, a John Deere 4250 like this one commanded a purchase price of $50,000. It offered a lot in return, such as an advanced 26-gallon-per-minute outlet flow hydraulic system; a dual-speed, independent PTO; and optional four-wheel-drive. Its power lift could handle 6,290 pounds. *Voyageur Press Archives*

With a host of valuable features, including a constant-mesh, 16-speed transmission, a 6,000-pound power lift, and 26-gallon-per-minute outlet flow hydraulics, the Model 4450 commanded a sticker price of $54,000 in 1988. *Voyageur Press Archives*

Model 4250 1983–1988

Engine:	Six-cylinder diesel-turbo
Displacement:	466 ci
Power:	121 PTO horsepower
Transmission:	Sixteen-speed forward
Weight:	11,200 pounds

A fine example of the Mannheim factory's work is this Model 2550, with its 56-drawbar-horsepower, four-cylinder diesel, and optional power shift transmission. *Voyageur Press Archives*

Model 2350 (Mannheim-Built) 1983–1986	
Engine:	Four-cylinder diesel
Bore & Stroke:	4.19x4.33 inches
Displacement:	239 ci
Power:	56 PTO horsepower
Transmission:	Twelve-speed forward
Weight:	6,500 pounds

For just $22,000 in 1986, you could own this German-made tractor with its 2,735-pound power lift, independent dual-speed PTO, and 13-gallon-per-minute hydraulics. *Voyageur Press Archives*

This Model 2350 demonstrated some of Deere's modern engineering prowess. It could turn a tight circle because of the front wheels' ability to tilt the tractor's plane of rotation by 13 degrees—essentially the 2350 could lean into a turn like a motorcycle. It came in a wide-tread version for vegetable farmers. *Voyageur Press Archives*

Built at the turn of the new century, the Model 6510 was made in Germany with a 95-PTO horsepower, four-cylinder turbo diesel rated at 2,300 rpm. It weighed 8,000 pounds. *Voyageur Press Archives*

Model 6500 1995–1997	
Engine:	Four-cylinder diesel-turbo
Displacement:	239 ci
Power:	95 PTO horsepower
Transmission:	Twelve-speed forward

The 6500L, part of Deere's "All New Breed of Power," was built in Germany between 1995 and 1997. It had a 239-cubic-inch turbo diesel and a Synchro transmission. *Voyageur Press Archives*

This 6400L, shown here with its John Deere 640A loader raised high, was built at Deere's Mannheim factory between 1992 and 1998. It had an optional four-wheel-drive and PowrQuad transmission, with 16 gears forward and 12 reverse. *Voyageur Press Archives*

The Model 7405 was introduced by Deere in the mid-1990s as a six-cylinder turbo-diesel tractor that could pump out more than 100 horsepower. It is pictured here with a Model 856 cultivator. *Voyageur Press Archives*

The 7800 was a high-horsepower tractor (146 at the PTO) that came out of Deere's Waterloo plant in the early 1990s. In its final year of production, it sold for $84,000. *Voyageur Press Archives*

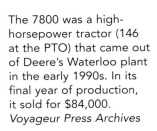

This is a two-wheel-drive version of the Model 7200 at left, built in the mid-1990s at the Waterloo plant. It has a 92-horsepower, six-cylinder turbo diesel. The engine displacement is 359 cubic inches. The model on the right is a 7400. *Voyageur Press Archives*

Model 7800 1992–1996

Engine:	Six-cylinder diesel-turbo
Bore & Stroke:	4.57x4.75 inches
Engine speed:	2,200 rpms
Displacement:	466 ci
Power:	146.73 PTO horsepower
Transmission:	Sixteen-speed forward

A big tractor with a lot of capability, the Model 8100 takes 135 gallons of diesel fuel and 28.8 quarts of oil. It has a three-point hitch and a 10,400-pound lift (with an optional extra boost to 14,165 pounds). Operating weight is close to nine tons.

Model 8100 1994–1998

Engine:	Six-cylinder diesel-turbo
Bore & Stroke:	4.56x5.06 inches
Engine speed:	2,200 rpms
Displacement:	496 ci
Power:	160 PTO horsepower
Transmission:	Sixteen-speed forward
Weight:	17,876 pounds

NEW 160-TO 225-HP 8000 SERIES TRACTORS
21st Century Technology Today

Above: The Model 8400 was powered by a six-cylinder, 496-cubic-inch (8.1 L) turbo diesel that delivered a whopping 225 horsepower to the PTO. It had a ground clearance of 23.2 inches, a wheelbase of just under 10 feet, and an operating weight of 18,709 pounds. The 8400 in this brochure has a 2550 disc attached. *Voyageur Press Archives*

The 8000 Series hit the dealerships in 1994 with horsepower to spare and the catchy tagline of "21st Century Technology Today." *Voyageur Press Archives*

The distinguishing feature of this 8410T series tractor is its set of rubber tracks, which reduce soil compaction and aid traction in slippery conditions. Produced between 1999 and 2002 at the Waterloo tractor works, the 8410T features a six-cylinder, 496-cubic-inch turbo diesel, rated at 829 ft-lbs of torque at 2,200 rpm.

This rubber-tracked 8410T has Deere's popular PowerShift transmission with 16 gears forward, and four in reverse, and its closed-center hydraulic system produces 30 gallons of hydraulic oil flow per minute. The tractor weighs more than 18,000 pounds, with a wheelbase of just under 10 feet.

It's not the similarities that upset our competitors . . .

NEW 136 to 191 kW (185 to 260 hp) John Deere 8000T Series Tractors

A brochure for the 8000T Series tractors that refers to Deere's move to put rubber tracks on field tractors.
Voyageur Press Archives

The Model 9400 is a fine example of Deere & Company's modern-day capabilities. The tractor's closed-center pump hydraulics have the tremendous flow rate of 44 gallons per minute, capable of performing a variety of functions around the machine. The 9400 comes standard with a mechanical lift rated to 13,871 pounds and an independent PTO.

Model 9300 1996–2002	
Engine:	Six-cylinder diesel-turbo
Bore & Stroke:	5.00x6.50 inches
Engine speed:	2,100 rpms
Displacement:	766 ci
Power:	317 drawbar horsepower
Transmission:	Twelve-speed forward
Weight:	31,440 pounds

A tool for large farming operations, this 360-horsepower Model 9300 applies enormous force in the field with its 766-cubic-inch (12.6L) turbo diesel. It has 620/70R42 tires front and rear, a 270-gallon fuel tank, and a working weight of over 31,000 pounds. Three batteries provide 2,775 cold-cranking amps.

A Model 9400 gets cleaned up. Built between 1996 and 2002 at the Waterloo factory, the 9400's six-cylinder, 766-cubic-inch turbo diesel produces a 371-horsepower tug at the drawbar. *Voyageur Press Archives*

INDEX